CRAFTSMEN
OF
WISCONSIN

CRAFTSMEN
OF
WISCONSIN
by Bertha Kitchell Whyte

Western Publishing Company, Inc. Racine, Wisconsin

ACCREDITATIONS

In preparing this book which describes the work of a mere dozen or so of Wisconsin's many fine craftsmen, I wish to acknowledge the cooperation of those I have known personally, especially Wesley Jung, Erhardt Stoetner, Emil Klingler, John Gaar and John Kane. William Te Ronde, deceased, whom I knew best of all, is included as the type of rugged individualist who was a sort of universal craftsman and would never have considered himself "copy."

In writing the introduction I was assisted by Guido Brink, artist and lately sculptor, who came from Dusseldorf, Germany, to work in stained glass for his uncle in New York City and for many years has taught painting at Layton Art School in Milwaukee. We had long discussions about the definition of craftsmanship in relation to folk art, sculpture, pure art.

Mr. Carl Moebius assisted me editorially, with advice from certain staff members of the Milwaukee Public Museum.

The book has been designed by Fred Hausman of Stamford, Conn., and printed by Western Publishing Company, Inc., Racine, Wisconsin.

Bertha K. Whyte

Contents

Preface

This book is of value to those who will read it because much of it is based on first hand observation either of the craftsmen themselves or those that lived in close association with them. The reader will get a clear feeling of a time not too long past. Much will jar the memory of the older readers or stir the vague memories of the not so old. The real value is that this information has been assembled, recorded, and is presented here to any that are curious enough to take the time to share it.

The recent past is all too soon forgotten. People and events of the previous generation gradually settle into a haze of disinterest and apathy. Two generations into the past is a point of nearly complete darkness.

When things are about one hundred years old they are called antique and people once again are interested in them and attach value to them. Once a thing has value, we wish to know what is this object, who made it, how it was made, where it was made, and what use was made of it. Too often the research to find answers to these questions are hampered because most of the records have been destroyed or lost. Legend or pure invention may provide a satisfying but untrue answer to any or all of the questions. Only the real student demands an answer based on facts. The author of this book is a real scholar who has searched for truth.

First hand experiences are of real value. A record of the recollections of a person about his own life, though veiled by time, are valid sets of facts. Observations about someone that was known in one's youth may be limited by the point of view of the observer but also are of value. Both of these types of information are offered in this book. The serious collector either private or museum will generally also seek out advertising, catalogues, patents and any existing records as solid ground on which to build a really clear understanding of a product, and the world in which it was created. This type of source material was also used in assembling this book.

The word craftsman suggests a creative force. Manual dexterity alone is not implied. The worker has learned his skill and its limitations and then using these talents innovates a product that reflects his unique qualities.

Each of the artisans covered in this book either had or has this unique creative drive. Out of the great mass of material produced in their time, their works should continue to be recognized as exceptional. Even if time and man are cruel enough to destroy most of the works of these craftsmen, this book will make it impossible for them to be lost forever to history. Through this book we can gain an insight into the driving force of each of these personalities.

Lastly and of equal importance, this book clearly reflects the tireless inquiring nature of the author. Her enthusiastic research and writing has created a product that is as much a part of her as any product made by the craftsmen treated in this book.

John W. Luedtke
Acting Curator of History
Milwaukee Public Museum

Introduction to Craftsmen of Wisconsin

At first, it might seem simple to define the word "craftsman," but in the attempt, one encounters many pitfalls. How is one to distinguish between a piece of primitive art, folk art, or the result of a hobby? Primitive art may go beyond craftsmanship, and influence sophisticated artists as African art influenced Picasso. Primitiveness may be art or may not. Sometimes folk art attains the status of real art; hobbies practically never.

The definition of art is very hard to give; in fact almost impossible. To say that when the element of design enters in, then the piece is a work of art, is not enough. It must be innovative in a creative sense. Often folk art has a spontaneity lacking in the fine arts. In the Bauhaus of Germany the members developed craft as an art. Edward Higgins[1] says, "There is no line between

[1] *Contemporary Sculpture* by Edward Higgins

fine arts and crafts today. Competence in craft and technique frees the artist to make the broadest and most specific statement."

Wisconsin craftsmen were of diverse origin and either brought their training from Continental Europe or developed it here from necessity. The reason why a few of them are still practicing their crafts is due to their genuine instincts and independent spirit; but such craftsmen, with the exception of stained glass workers, are dying out. This is unfortunate because the handmade object has a beauty of its own. Machine made furniture, for instance, does not ordinarily have the charm or durability of good, hand-made pieces which are, consequently, so eagerly sought after.

What is a craft? As I have already stated, there is no strict line today between fine arts and crafts. The difference seems blurred, and in relationship of the one to the other, overlappings often occur. For instance, ceramics is a craft, although generally considered an art today. William Morris, the English Pre-Raphaelite designer, best known for the Morris chair, advises, "Have nothing in your house that you do not know to be useful, or believe to be beautiful." Whereas crafts are primarily for use, the fine arts are to contemplate, and to enjoy. The basic characteristic that both art and craft have in common, is that of having been brought into being, through the specific and creative power of man. "More than anything else" Bernard S. Meyers[2] has observed, "what impels us to differentiate between major and minor arts is the latter's lack of spiritual significance or deeper meaning. Yet with crafts their aim is sometimes either functional, or a combination of the two." Without art, crafts can be very dull; some examples deteriorate into the status of souvenirs.

Fundamentally, a craftsman is a workman whose product is made with a maximum of skill, directed to a useful object, but

[2] Bernard S. Myers, Henry Holt & Co.

in certain cases one would say of their products, "They are works of art." The real craftsman's work is more than a therapeutic hobby. It is not folk art which develops from generations of practice by untrained peoples using traditional designs. Nevertheless, folk art may have a spontaneity lacking in the fine arts. The work of Per Lysne, the distinguished rosemaler of Stoughton, Wisconsin, might qualify as folk art, although his execution was almost too highly skilled to be folk art, trained as he was by his father in Norway. Other craftsmen in Wisconsin are European trained workers who learned their trade in work shops which had practised special crafts for hundreds of years. Others were self taught. The craftsman was an individual with creative instincts who took useful objects and made them beautiful. The spirit of these men is reflected in their grace and dedication to their work, which endures in its beauty.

Jacques Maritain[3] remarks, "Finally, to sum up, let us say that in the useful arts, what the will or appetite demands is a satisfying of a particular need."

Our older craftsmen that we are about to introduce produced things which were not only useful but were often beautiful as well. Visits to the studios of these artisans of philosophical character were, and in a few remaining instances are, old fashioned pleasures greatly to be enjoyed.

[3] *Creative Intuition in Art and Poetry*, by Jacques Maritain-A. W. Mellon Lectures, Bollingen series, In the Fine Arts, National Gallery of Art. Washington, 1953.

I
John Gaar,
Master
Cabinet Maker

JOHN GAAR,
MASTER CABINET MAKER

Milwaukee was fortunate in having John Gaar immigrate to the city from Neudau, Steirmark, Austria in 1929 with his wife and son John. Joe, Mary and the twins, Leo and Michael, were born in Milwaukee and in due time attended St. John's High School, walking from their home on Franklin Place. Mr. Gaar's shop was for many years on Ogden Avenue, but when his business became extensive he moved to a brick house on nearby Curtis Place. In

John Gaar with his co-worker son, Joseph.

(page 14) John Gaar at his workshop in his converted barn in Brookfield.

1949 he moved to a small farm at 2480 Pilgrim Road in Brook-field, far enough away so that patrons could not dump truck loads of antique finds on his crowded space. He had been brought so many pieces which did not merit his expert repair.

There was a barn on the farm with a cement foundation two feet thick, left when the barn was torn down and on which they themselves erected, in 1950, a shop, and above that a chalet type house of one story. The shop utilized the eastern slope.

Three of the boys were drafted in World War II; two of them were wounded, and Leo was drafted afterwards. Mary married and moved to California where her children enjoyed the doll beds and toys made and sent by their grandfather. Michael was the only brother to be married, but John Jr., and Joe were so beautifully trained in cabinet work that they have worked with their father professionally from the beginning, and now that John Gaar, Sr., has retired, due to a sawdust allergy, they carry on a business in which they always report "too much work."

The remarkable feature of these cabinet makers is the expert-ise which they exhibit. John Jr., who had worked with his grand-father in Austria, is a very fine wood carver. All three did fine inlay work, especially John Gaar Sr., who labored painstakingly over Dutch and French marquetry antiques which had been brought from abroad and had deteriorated in American central heating. These craftsmen made perfect reproductions; unrecog-nizable duplicates of original pieces, which displayed the finest of workmanship.

Gilbert Pelham came to Milwaukee from New York on an appraisal mission and, on seeing John Gaar's work, declared that it had been done with maximum skill. But John Gaar could de-sign too, as he did for my family, both in mahogany and pine. He made a low oval shaped inlaid table to fit a tray, as well as some office furniture for my husband.

(page 16) Chippendale lowboy, by John Gaar, from the collection of the Frederick Heidners.

18

As a trainee, John Gaar was apprenticed to his father and obtained his experience working on the furniture of various castles, chiefly, Castel *Schloss Neudau*, whose owner was Excellenz Adelbert Graf Kotolinsky of the Hapsburg Camera. He worked a year and a half at this castle and a half year at *Schloss Offanberg*, besides a time at *Schloss Weyer*. In these castles some of the furniture was five hundred years old. Like Isaac Sack of New York, who could tell what kind of wood it was by the feel of it, John Gaar had precious knowledge of woods.

He still has some of the tools he had brought from Neudau, including a chisel for making tongue and grooving, his old plane, and a drill for making dowel holes. One of our pieces he worked on was an ancient organ clock or Concerto Walzer, dated 1649, with a music box which played eight tunes, among which was "*O du lieber Augustine.*" The signature was "Johan Sifert, Neustadt."

(above) Small pipe organ and top of the bellows of the organ clock, dated 1648. (In the author's collection.)

(page 18) Small Hepplewhite sideboard by John Gaar, in the Collection of Dr. and Mrs. Frederick C. Heidner, Milwaukee.

There are 28 Neustadts in Central Europe, among them, Steir-mark Neustadt.

John Gaar testified that the granulation of the finish indicated that the clock was at least 200 years old and that the case was Gothic in style, having been altered, perhaps. He also said that the veneer was hand sawn and a quarter of an inch thick. He thought that the clock had come originally from the home of

(above) The clock in Lake Mills, before restoration.

(page 21) The clock in Milwaukee, after being completely restored.

a wealthy land owner, although it was of a primitive type. The wood was cherry with curly maple veneer. At the top of the clock above the face, appears a small balcony with five little wooden musicians dressed in Swiss costumes who play their instruments and move automatically while the music box is playing. A fifty pound iron weight runs the music box and bellows for the pipe organ; a twenty-five pound weight ran the clock. The paintings on the face depict William Tell shooting Gessler, and on top there is a sleeping lion and a red cross.

John Gaar finished the case; John Davis of Lake Mills restored the clock; Joseph Shaefer of Slinger tuned up the music box. Twenty-five years ago all was in working order, but the works were too ancient to keep it up and now all is intact, but quiet.

At the time of writing this sketch, John Gaar is very ill and the two cabinet making sons of this gentle family are unable to cope with the clients who "beat a path to their door." In fact, they plead for no mention for that reason. The low wooden shop where I first knew them was a few doors away from Thatcher's Drug Store on the corner of Farwell and Ogden Avenues (and a regular institution and first aid center for removing cinders from eyes.) Across was Abbot Row, about which many stories have been written. It was a cooperative row of ten connected houses where many prominent Milwaukee families have lived.* Practically all of these had Gaar pieces.

But now the county plans to gouge a path for an expressway through that area and all will be changed. At any rate, old time craftmanship such as the Gaar's is definitely on the wane, for scarcer and scarcer are expert shoemakers, upholsterers, furriers, needleworkers, stone carvers and above all, cabinet makers. We can be counted lucky that of the latter, Milwaukee has had one of the best.

(page 22) Game table as a gift for the author, by John Gaar. The squares are of mahogany and satinwood. (Furniture photographs by Richard Eels, of Milwaukee.)

* The John Cudahys (He was ambassador to Poland and Belgium), the Samuel Butlers (long head of the Art Institute), the William D. Van Dyke Juniors, the William A. Norrises, the Edmund Sheas, the Richard Joneses, the Rudy Matthews, the Henry Reusses (he is member of the U.S. House of Representatives), the Heber Stouts, the Donald Slichters, the Serge Troubetzkoys, Irving Mantey and Miss Dorothy Brown.

II
Rosemaler
Per Lysne of Stoughton

ROSEMALER PER LYSNE OF STOUGHTON

A craftsman of Norwegian origin is Per Lysne, who was born in Laerdal, Sogn, Norway, in 1880. He received his training as a rosemaler or flower painter under his father, who had been awarded a bronze medal in the Paris Exposition in 1898. To illustrate the extent of his father's operation, Mrs. Nundahl of Stoughton, a sister of Per Lysne, told of her recollection of furniture decorated by her father being crated and shipped to England.

Rosemaling is the decorative art of rose painting which developed in Scandinavian countries and flourished for a hundred years or more. In early times the painting was done in relation to carving in the rooms of houses or in churches. Decorated carved ale bowls from the 16th and 17th centuries seem to have been the inspiration for rosemaling in Norway.

(page 26) Alfred Lunt and Lynn Fontanne (with Clagett Wilson), decorating their first home in Genesee Depot, Wisconsin. The date is some time in the thirties. Picture from the scrapbook of Mrs. Osborne Lysne.

27

Young Lysne emigrated to Stoughton, Wisconsin, on September 1, 1906, when he was twenty-six years old. He lived there until his death at the age of sixty seven in 1947. In Sogn, Per Lysne had helped his father decorate churches, but in Stoughton his first job was as a striper, painting wheels and bodies in the Mandt Wagon Works. As time and the depression decreased employment at the wagon shop, Lysne turned to rosemaling smorgasbords in his own shop, with smorgasbord plates turned

Photograph of Per Lysne of Stoughton, Wisconsin.

out by Andrew Kvalheim and Donovan Wake. These had originated in Sweden (as unpainted wooden platters), but in painting them, Lysne used traditional Norwegian designs on white or light yellow backgrounds. Eventually he was responsible for the revival of rosemaling in Wisconsin and, in fact, throughout the United States.

A letter to Per Lysne from Mrs. Nora Edmunds of the American Friends of Norway, Inc., in New York, is quoted as follows:

"I have been wanting to write you for some time to thank you for the wonderful work you did for the cause of Norway at Christmas time. We most deeply appreciated your sending so many Smorgasbordet platters to us. They were unques-

Design of Per Lysne from the collection of Osborne Lysne.

tionably one of the most popular things in the shop during the holiday season. Several people came into the shop who knew your work and some who knew you personally. They told us that you had decided to give us your entire output. We wish to thank you in the name of Norway for your wonderful help.

Had I known you were going to be so generous with us, I would have put the Smorgasbordet platter in our Christmas booklet. It would have been a huge success by mail. Could I count on your giving us as many platters next Chirstmas

Chest dated 1794 of the Lysne family, repainted by Per Lysne.

as you did this Christmas as I would like to feature it in our booklet if you would let me? I would use your name as I think this would mean a great deal to Norwegians all over the country. Could you, for instance, give us two hundred platters by October 1st—all large, if possible, and all with the green leaf design as this is by far the most saleable? I could not illustrate all the different designs and people always want what they see in the picture.

One of Per Lysne's specialties was redecorating antique chests which had been brought over from Norway. It has been estimated that he decorated 600 of these during his career, all of which are now preserved as cherished items. At first he did his own carpentering of jorestals (three-legged chairs). Later he enlisted the help of Haaken Thole, a cabinet maker of Stoughton, so that he could devote himself exclusively to the rosemaling art.

In the Renaissance, geometric designs with zig zag borders were common. Viking interweaving was also used. Baroque scroll forms based on the acanthus leaf were popular throughout Europe in the 18th century and were incorporated into the rosemaling designs also. In Sweden, designs had more figures, animals, and realistic flowers than in Norway, where the flower designs were more imaginary and stylized.

In Folk Arts of Norway[1] Janice Stewart comments:
"The vine or leaf forms in some variation carried through the whole rosemaling period with the rococo line increasingly evident in later years. Flower motifs continue to be used but in such imaginative decorative form that their prototypes would be impossible to find. Some Telemark flowers looked shell-like and were probably suggested by the rococo shell motif of the Louis XV period."
Although Per Lysne could tell from which province an object came by the design with which it was painted, his designs were

[1] Folk Arts of Norway, Janice Stewart, University of Wisconsin Press.

His father's trunk, restored by Per Lysne in the Museum in Stoughton. Note the date, *1854*, forged in iron band in the center of the trunk lid. Owner, Bjarne Lysne. Photographer, Art Wendt, Stoughton, Wisconsin.

all original and freely painted.[2,3] He used no stencils, but carefully made a design appropriate to the piece to be painted, then worked directly upon it freehand. He never allowed his pupils to copy his designs.

Per Lynse did not drive or own a car but followed the Norwegian custom of living in the homes he was decorating because he liked to have people around him while he was painting. He decorated the homes of Martin P. Paulson (now owned by John Best) in Elm Grove, where Lysne worked for three weeks, of

Chairs painted by Per Lysne for Mrs. William D. Hoard, Fort Atkinson, Wisconsin. Note tine box on chairs. Photograph by Mrs. Hoard.

[2] Two books on *Rosemaling* have been written by Wisconsin writers; one by Bjarne and Harriet Romnes was published in 1966 by the Norwegian-American Museum of Decorah, Iowa; and the other by Gladys H. Fossum was published in Racine, Wisconsin, in 1964 as a Glicksum Book. Mrs. Romnes' father worked as a cabinetmaker and wood carver with Per Lysne and she became one of Lysne's pupils. The Romnes instituted the first Wisconsin regional exhibition of rosemaling at their Chalet Gardens in Madison in May, 1967.
[3] In the two volumes of design by Anne Foote and Elaine Smedal, one in 1946, *Norwegian Design in Wisconsin*, and one in 1948, *Decorative Art in Wisconsin*, beautifully serigraphed and published by The Campus Publishing Company of the University of Wisconsin, no mention was made of the craftsman, Per Lysne, who was restoring the art of rosemaling in Wisconsin after it had languished in Norway itself. Evidently these authors have restricted themselves to designs and articles "brought along" as antiques from Norway.

Dr. Herman Schumm on Oconomowoc Lake, Doctors Fred Madison and Frederick Heidner in Milwaukee. He also did the kitchens of the Raymond Zillmer home in Wauwatosa and the Bjarne Romnes home in Madison.

Kitchen of the Frederick Heidners by Per Lysne.

The painting of the Zillmer kitchen in March of 1935, took about ten days; Mr. Lysne working free-hand but consulting his designs and adding some German mottos on request. A varnish was added later. Mrs. Zillmer described Per Lysne as a very quiet, gentle man whom they enjoyed very much.

(page 34) Kubestal, three legged chair, decorated by Per Lysne in the collection of his son, Osborne Lysne. Photo by Elmer Richardson.

The home of the most famous persons where Per Lysne did rosemaling was that of Alfred Lunt and Lynn Fontanne in Genesee. Their first cottage had been fashioned from two chicken houses by architect Carl Dornbusch. The general decor was Swedish; the kitchen was done by Claggett Wilson of New York and the living room by Alfred Lunt himself. Pieces by Per Lysne in the guest room were shown in an article in *Vogue Magazine* of November, 1933. According to a letter from Mr. Lunt, to me, in August, 1966, "The only pieces of furniture in the cottage at Genesee that were painted by a Norwegian (he did come from Stoughton) are two chairs and a kitchen cupboard. There were two doors on a wardrobe but they have since been destroyed. The walls are Swedish and not done by Lysne."

Per Lysne recounted to his son, Osborne, the scene of his painting in Genesee. While he was busy painting, Alfred Lunt was making borscht in the kitchen, and Lynn Fontanne was practicing her lines before their dog. Earlier Lysne remembered Alfred Lunt in 1929 driving into Stoughton in a Model "A" Ford to visit the fall harvest festival, but due to his famous friend's desire for anonymity, Per Lysne never disclosed Mr. Lunt's identity.

Distinctive celebrations are held twice a year in Stoughton. The May 17th Norwegian Independence Day is still celebrated, at which time the Per Lysne smorgasbords are carried in the parades. On all festival days, examples of his work can be seen in the interesting Stoughton Museum, which is housed in what was once the old Universalist Church, where ladies in Norwegian costumes act as guides on festival days. At such times the church would serve Norwegian food and the stores would feature Norwegian antiques.

Per Lysne had written poetry in Norway; he never drank but had been a worker for temperance and Norwegian cultural groups. The charming custom of employing mottos as decoration on walls, tines, smorgasbords was followed by Per Lysne, script and

Norwegian festival celebrated on the 17th day of May (the Norwegian Fourth of July), featuring examples of Lysne rosemaling in the parade, Stoughton, Wisconsin.

Kitchen decorated by Per Lysne for the Raymond Zillmer home in Wauwatosa. The motto reads, "Wer seine Arbeit fleissig tut, dem schmeckt auch seine Suppe gut." Photograph by Richard Eells.

Gothic lettering being used in Norwegian, never in English. The sayings were simple expressions of hospitality, such as one owned by Mrs. Lester O. Peterson formerly of Stoughton, "A sumptuous spread is laid out upon the table so won't you come and help yourself?"

Others are:

"Smorgasbord is now set. Help yourself."

"Hunger is der beste Koch."

"He who does his work industriously, to him supper will also taste good."

"Gruss Gott Guten Morgen."

"Wer seine Arbeit fleissig tut, dem schmeckt auch seine Suppe gut."

Room decorated by Per Lysne for the Bjarnes Romnes' home, now that of Mr. & Mrs. John Best in Brookfield, Wisconsin.

"Gott segne unser Haus."

"In a hundred years everything is forgotten."

"Each day has its own cares."

Madison is the setting of a story illustrating the modest nature of our craftsman on the occasion of the visit of the Crown Prince of Norway on June 19–20, 1939. The Crown Prince sent a messenger to Stoughton to invite Per Lysne to visit him, but Lysne felt that such an honor was too great to accept and declined. His modesty belied the extent of his national recognition. On one occasion an autograph seeker came to Wisconsin in search of certain signatures of prominent citizens of the state. He wanted, among others, those of President Glen Frank of the University, the football coach Harry Stuhldreher, Green Bay Packer coach, E. L. (Curley) Lambeau, Frank Lloyd Wright, John Stuart Curry, August Derleth, Thornton Wilder, Leon Pescheret (Whitewater etcher), and Per Lysne.[1]

Many of the chests Per Lysne decorated are now at Little Norway, the Norwegian Museum near Blue Mound, Wisconsin. Two of his pupils were Mrs. Osborne Lysne, his daughter-in-law, and her mother. Another was the daughter of Haakon Thole, Mrs. Bjarne Romnes, who in turn taught rosemaling, and with her husband, operates Chalet Gardens, Madison, with its retirement home, gift shop and restaurant.

Besides the decoration of rooms and walls in Wisconsin, Per Lysne, with his painted dower chests, kubbestols (chairs made of hollowed out logs), band chairs, cupboards, tines (bent wood boxes used for cheese or butter) and smorgasbords, created a revival of folk art which had declined in Norway itself, but which has enriched the state and national scene with its color and design.

(opposite page) Bowl and smorgasbord of Mrs. Frederick O. Heidner, Milwaukee. Photograph by Richard Eells, Milwaukee.

1 Autographs, 1940 collected by Edwin A. Rowlands of Pittsburgh, Pa. See Journal Green Sheet, Dec. 5, 1940. Pictures of Lysne's plates appeared in the Saturday Evening Post, Better Homes and Gardens, and in Montgomery Ward's catalogue.

Smørgaasbordet er nu dækket—Vær saa god!

III
Harry Nohr
Maker of Bowls

HARRY NOHR
MAKER OF BOWLS

In the picturesque city of Mineral Point in Southwestern Wisconsin where Robert Neal and Edgar Hellum have labored for thirty-five years restoring the stone cottages built by Cornish miners who came to mine lead and zinc around 1838, there is a craftsman who makes beautiful wooden bowls. His name is Harry Nohr and he was born in 1897 in Waupaca, Wisconsin, of Danish emigrant parents.

His first craftsmanship was in France when, as a soldier in World War I, he made and sold vases (out of brass shells). They were elaborately chased against the shell inserted in the casing (after the ammunition was removed) with the use of tools made out of German gun parts and those from French airplanes. He had had an eighth grade education.

(page 44) Harry Nohr in his workshop in the process of cutting a bowl.

Back in Wisconsin he started in as a butter and ice cream maker but from 1949 to 1966 he was the postmaster of Mineral Point. Since 1925, members of the Nohr family have lived in a large, white-painted home at 307 High Street which was built in 1870 on the basis of two rooms which are over a hundred years old. This capacious house, which is given over to the making and showing of bowls, has no screen porches because there is no marshland near Mineral Point in which mosquitoes can generate, this being the driftless area of Wisconsin. Harry Nohr lives there now with his wife, both of whom are confirmed nature lovers. Inside the house are trophies of the hunt and outside bird feeders of many descriptions. He buys sunflower seed in ten, fifty pound sacks at a time and the same amount of cracked corn, 500 pounds of each.

As my driver and I took breakfast with the Nohrs in August, 1969, we were eating the same strawberry jam which young birds were enjoying just outside the window in a special container.

It was in 1959 that Mr. Nohr took up wood turning, which time-consuming occupation takes his entire time in the days of his retirement, and after much experimentation he made his first bowl. The process which finally evolved was his own and is not likely to be soon followed, although Mr. Nohr is willing to give instructions.

First he cuts down a chosen tree. Then he cuts out a bowl-shaped block with a band saw, coats it with wax, wraps it in newspaper and stores it with many others in a basement room under exact control as to temperature and humidity. There it stays for two years to season.

After being unwrapped, the block is then cut by hand on a lathe with a very hard steel tool which produces fine shavings and a bowl of the uniform thickness of one-eighth of an inch. That is the point where craftsmanship, patience and a steady

Harry Nohr's house in
Mineral Point.

Harry Nohr with bowl blocks before cutting.

47

hand are necessary. Some bowls take nine hours of continuous cutting, during which his wife brings a sandwich for luncheon and he listens to music and gets an education from lectures coming over WHA, the University of Wisconsin radio station. He also plays records and at the final cutting he needs low music; preferably by Fritz Kreisler on the violin, or Wayne King on the saxophone. He says this helps him have a steady hand.

After the turning is finished the bowl is baked in Mrs. Nohr's oven at about 200 degrees for six hours, for it must be absolutely dry to procure deep penetration of the epoxy, a synthetic polyester which Mr. Nohr gets in Sheboygan. This epoxy is passed by the Department of Agriculture as safe for food, but must be used in brushing with a mask and rubber gloves behind a big fan. He generally brushes thirty bowls at a time, using one thin and then three heavy coats. After drying, there comes about three hours of hand rubbing on an average size bowl—first with silicon carbide abrasive paper; next with flowers of pumice stone and steel wool followed by rotten stone. These rubbings take off the epoxy shine and bring out the beautiful wood patterns and develop a soft glow to the colors.

When the bowls are finished "one can use anything in them but fuming nitric acid," says Mr. Nohr; hot or cold dishes, punch and flowers. The epoxy adds great strength to the bowl. They do not break easily. They can be put in electric dishwashers. He sells his work at Art Fairs in places such as Racine, Milwaukee, Madison, and La Crosse, but mostly at his home, and is always short in supply.

Mr. Nohr uses woods from more than twenty native trees, but also some rare woods as pecan from Florida, monkey pod

(page 48) Harry Nohr with a finished bowl behind a stump fitted with corncobs for birds.

from Hawaii and ailanthus. He uses black, burr, red and white oak. Fiddle back maple is cut from birdseye maple but cut parallel to the eye. The following is a list of native trees used by Mr. Nohr:

Ironwood
Butternut
Shagbark Hickory
Walnut
Apple
Birds Eye Maple
Cherry
Catalpa

Red Elm
Ginkgo
Kentucky Coffee Bean
Yellow Birch
Red Birch
Black, red, burr and white oak
Hard Maple
Silver Maple

Linden
Sumac
Black Ash
Hackberry
Box Elder
Black Locust
Golden Willow

He has a special collection of bowls made from burls of most of these trees. Mr. Nohr has won awards at Wisconsin Designer

Craftsmen Show, Wisconsin State Fair, Wisconsin Regional Art Shows and other Art Fairs and shows. He has bowls on a world tour with Objects, U.S.A. sponsored by the Johnson Wax Company of Racine, Wisconsin. The American Broadcasting Company has distributed an hour television program called "With These Hands" featuring special craftsmen of the United States one of whom was Harry Nohr. The program emphasized the resurgence of craftsmenship which is now taught in hundreds of educational institutions.

Mr. Harry Nohr was honored on "Cultural Wisconsin Day" by the University of Wisconsin for "the high quality of his creative work and the many contributions he has made towards a broader interest in art," in 1965.

He served on the Wisconsin Conservation Congress and was on its Executive Council and is vitally interested in the state's wild life and its preservation.

In his pursuit of a hobby, Harry Nohr produced an art in the rhythm and swirls of wood graining and a lucrative vocation, as well. In comparing his bowls with those sold in the Virgin Isles (probably made in Haiti) and those of redwood in California, I find that his bowls, being thin and the wood more polished, are more varied and more beautiful, besides having more varied uses.

page 50) Photograph of Nohr bowls by Edgar Odma of Dodgeville, Wisconsin.

IV
Instrument Craftsman
E. F. Klingler

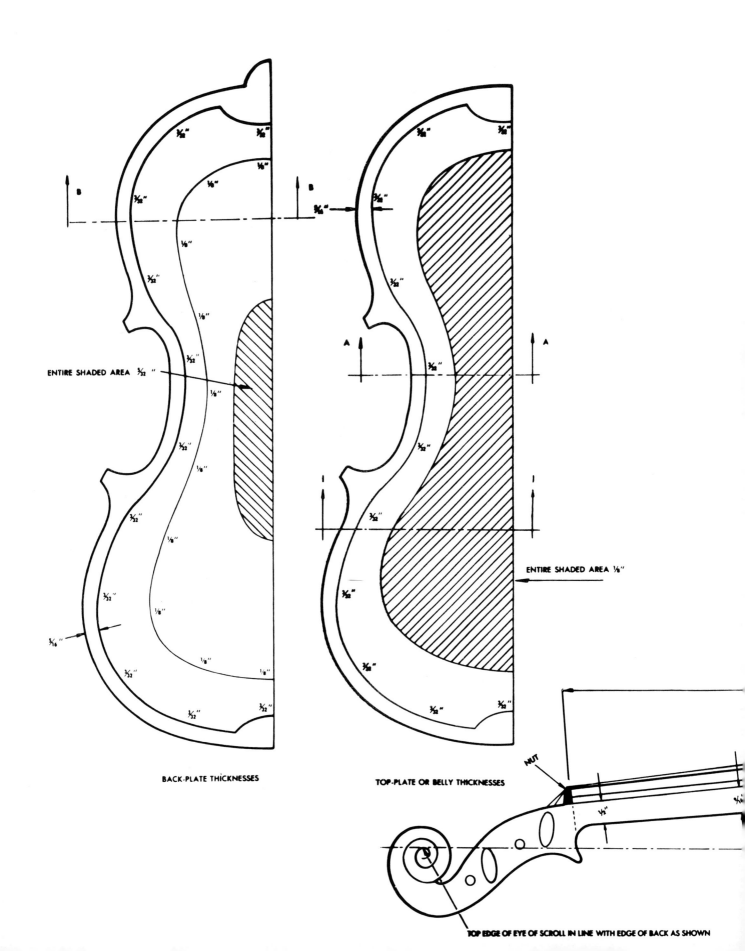

ENTIRE SHADED AREA ⁵⁄₃₂"

ENTIRE SHADED AREA ⅛"

BACK-PLATE THICKNESSES

TOP-PLATE OR BELLY THICKNESSES

NUT

TOP EDGE OF EYE OF SCROLL IN LINE WITH EDGE OF BACK AS SHOWN

INSTRUMENT
CRAFTSMAN
E. F. KLINGLER

As a craftsman in stringed instrument repair (violin, viola, cello and bass viol), Emil F. Klingler of Eau Claire, Wisconsin, developed from the age of eight when he played the violin at country and public dances with his father until he became a carpenter at the age of fifteen. From a carpenter he became a saw mill and woodwork factory operator where he got his start in architecture reading blueprints and specifications for millwork. With the aid of a set of books, studied during winter months, he developed into an architect, licensed to practice in the State of Wisconsin.

Throughout his whole career, after ending his formal education at the 6th grade, he was self-taught except in the case of learning to play the harp when he took forty lessons at the age

Diagrams of violins.

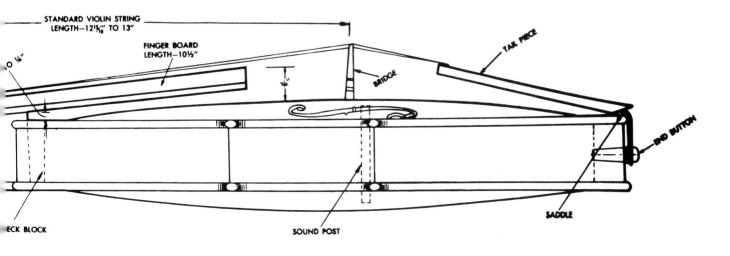

of seventy and first learned then to read notes. Although he played string instruments during his whole life, it was always by ear and from memory, aided by a sense of pitch.

During my interview with him in Eau Claire on September 22, 1965, he played on the violin the "theme song" with which he and his father started during their dance programs back in the nineties. He was then, at the time of our interview, 77, and also played a composition on his harp. The rooms in the basement of his large Victorian home at 715 Third Avenue, where he re-

Home of Klingler in Eau Claire. His shop is in the basement.

paired instruments, stored his valuable collection of old violins, books on violins and architecture, and early Wisconsin history, were in highly professional order. Although he is still President of E. F. Klingler & Associates, Inc., an architectural firm of 15–18 members, his main interest now is the repair and adjustment of bow playing string instruments in his basement shop.

(page 56) Mr. Klingler, as of 1970, besides his repair of school instruments, has been working on those of the Minneapolis and Eau Claire symphony orchestries.

(100) Ancient violin shop in Mittenwald, Bayern, Germany, which has been the center of violin manufacturers since 1680.

How well his work shop compares with an ancient one in Mittenwald, Bavaria (shown here).

In 1925 Mr. Klingler made a fine looking violin, but decided that there was greater interest, challenge and satisfaction in restoring *old* violins. That is his business now and he is exceedingly busy, in good health, repairing instruments for various musicians and for high schools. He says that he sometimes works in his home shop until two in the morning. Mr. Klingler learned the fundamentals of repairing instruments from a family friend in Winona, Minnesota. In 1968, he located a fellow repairman who could take over his very active business in the event of an inability to carry on his activities. His choice was Mr. Howard Kraus of Ellsworth, a former farmer and field director of the Farmers Union, a violinist and self taught violin repairman. Emil Klingler tells his methods in repairing instruments in the following account:

"As for articles to be repaired, they come to my shop in all conditions and sizes—all sorts of violins, violas, cellos and

* Schones Bayern, Werner Meyer, Verlag Wolfgand Weidlich Frankfurt am Main.

double bass. Some come for refinishing, setting a sound post, replacing a bridge, refitting the ebony pegs, tuning the fingerboard, replacing from 1 to all 4 strings, repairing cracks on the top or bottom plate, or plates which may have become unglued from the ribs which is caused by keeping the instrument in a room with too much or too little humidity. Most of these can be repaired from the outside. However, if top or bottom plate becomes damaged, it requires removal of top or bottom plate, then the cracked or damaged part is repaired or replaced, and reinforced with small strips of the same material as the damaged piece, placed at right angle and across the damaged part, then trimmed and scraped very thin so as not to affect the tone. Later the repaired plate is glued back in place on the instrument with a good violin hide glue which can be bought from instrument supply houses in a granular or flake dry form. In order to prepare it, it must be soaked in clean cold water at least one hour in advance to being heated in a double compartment utensil to keep the glue from burning. The glue must be heated to a boil and the work done in a warm room, free from draft, so that it does not chill, then clamped into place and surplus glue cleaned away from exposed areas with a clean cloth dipped in hot water, and wiped with a dry cloth or it may have to be scraped off with a chance of ruining the finish.

Woods Used: Top plate is a fine close grain spruce, grown in a cold climate, preferably in altitudes of at least 10,000 feet. The back plate, neck and scroll, and the ribs are made of various woods. Hard or soft maple, cut quarter grain from logs, looking at the end of the log, appears to be pie shaped when cut ready to serve, which creates a beautiful flame or curly wood. The ribs are the thin pieces all around the instrument between the top and bottom plate. The plates may be in full widths or in two pieces, each matching the other in the center of plate, glued full length. Then the exterior is formed to proper shape and the inside is cut out to proper thickness which also varies in thickness, being heavier all along the outer edges, and a small portion through the center, then thinner between these points to provide a vibration.

The fingerboard is glued on the upper portion of the neck, the tailpiece placed at the lower end of the instrument, fastened to an end pin fitted through the rib to a block inside, and the pegs fitted through a peg box on the upper edge of the scroll to where the strings are supported. All these parts can be made of ebony, rosewood or boxwood. All wood shall be thoroughly dried in an air loft, free from moisture, from 15 to 25 years. Some of the inner parts of the sound post is also of spruce, fitted between top and bottom plate, set slightly back of bridge foot. The other foot sets at right angles over the base bar inside of the instrument. This bridge supports the strings stretched between the tailpiece and pegs to hold them at the proper height and spacing.

The tone is created by moving the hair of the bow at right angles over the strings. The hairs are kept well rosined so as to create a vibration which is transmitted to the top through the bridge. Then the vibration passes into the sound box, transferred to the back by way of sound posts, and dispersed throughout the chamber. It comes out through the sound holes on each end of the bridge, and the final results all depend on the selection of woods and proper gradation of plates, and the workmanship of the craftsman.

In the early days of the 1920s, such as in my days, all this was accomplished with suitable types of chisels, scrapers, hand saws, planes and sharp knives, whereas now, and for several years, machines cut all parts in much shorter time for construction of the cheaper instruments, but the better instruments are still being made with hand tools. The same applied to repairs. After the instrument is smoothly finished with very fine sandpaper, it is finished with some 8 or 10 coats of special oil or spirit colored varnish, each coat rubbed to a fine, velvet finish. The biggest dif-

Mr. Klingler's antique tool collection.

ficulty in repairs is to color the varnish to match the present finish, as well as applying same."

Mr. Klingler has probably the most interesting collection of violins in Wisconsin as well as in the Twin Cities area. In March, 1964,

(page 62) Left—No. 2 violin made by Gaspard Duiffoprugger in 1517, with carved scroll. The lower bout of wood is inlaid in various woods with scenes of churches, stone fences, and streets.

(page 63) Right is No. 5 violin, by Nicolius Simontre, in 1871. Note carving on scroll and carved portrait of Abraham Lincoln raised in an oval frame in the upper back bout.

he purchased 42 violins of the collection of Nels Remlin's estate of Red Wing, Minnesota, who died in January, 1963, at the age of 85. Eighteen violins of the Remlin collection had beautifully carved scrolls (heads); the Paganini alone was valued at $10,000. Mr. Remlin was active in his violin repair shop for over 33 years, but in his earlier days he headed a three piece dance band consisting of harp, played by Mr. Remlin, clarinet and violin. The violin player also played the drum set with one foot. They covered the northern central part of Wisconsin and Northeastern part of Minnesota. Mr. Klingler made it a practice to call on Mr. Remlin at least once or twice each year for his last ten years, finding him in his shop busy with repair work on violins.

As to the acquisition of the Remlin fine violin collection, Remlin's daughter could not give much information about his

Collection of violins for repair or sale.

business affairs (he was a loner), but Mr. Klingler was of the opinion that Nels Remlin apparently received them in his shop for repairs from 1942–1952. When the cost of repairs ran rather high, he either bought or took them in on reconditioned instruments. Some of them have their old original labels while others have only the Remlin Shop labels.

Besides the violins from Mr. Remlin in Red Wing, Minnesota, others in the Klingler collection came from Plymouth, Sheboygan, Ripon and Fond du Lac, Wisconsin, and one from Houston, Texas. The collection numbers 300 items and is valued at over $50,000. The rare examples may some day be bequeathed to the Eau Claire Wisconsin State University Fine Arts School Library, Eau Claire, Wisconsin.

Below is a list and description of Mr. Klingler's rarest and oldest violins:

No. 1 Violin: Beautiful Paganini violin, name engraved on back of scroll. The back and ribs have beautiful design work with an eagle in center of back. Label inside indicates it was acquired by Nels Remlin in Feburary, 1943. Wonderful tone and condition.

No. 2 Violin: Beautiful carved scroll and engraved rosettes on top and back plates at corners of C's. Ribs engraved with the following: GASTRO X NEMVS ARIES RESONAT FESV DEL PRIMA. Lower bout wood inlaid in various woods of soft colors to match finish. Scene of churches, stone fences, streets and all sorts of other buildings. Double row purfling. Also a coat of arms in upper bout. Label inside, Gaspard Duiffoprugger, bononienfis Anno 1517. Acquired by Nels Remlin in February, 1943, Excellent tone and condition.

No. 3 *Violin:* Beautiful carved scroll and wood inlaid scene on lower bout of back of various woods with matched finish. Label inside Gaspro da Salo, in Brescia. No date given. Acquired by Nels Remlin in February, 1943. Excellent tone and condition.

No. 4 *Violin:* Conventional scroll and top plate. Back contains beautiful biblical scenes in upper and lower bout, an angel in center bout, including all sorts of scenes all around on ribs. No maker's label. Acquired by Nels Remlin in February, 1958. Excellent tone and condition.

No. 5 *Violin:* Carving on side of scroll and beautiful carved portrait of Abraham Lincoln raised in an oval frame in the upper back bout. Label inside Nicolius Simontre, Lapot Nicoiai discipulus, Divoduri fecit 1871. Acquired by Nels Remlin in July, 1946. Excellent tone and condition.

No. 6 *Violin:* Beautiful double row purfling ornament in upper and lower bouts of top plate and upper, central and lower bouts on back plate. Inscription Jasilvis Viva Silure in upper bout. Canora, center bout, and jammortuacane in lower bout. Label inside Antonius Stradivarius Cremonenia Faciebat Anna 1724 F.
Another label reads: "When I was alive in the Woods, I was Silent. But now that I am dead I sing songs." Acquired by Nels Remlin in February, 1930. Excellent orange colored varnish finish, boxwood pegs, tailpiece, and end pin. Curly maple back and ribs and close grain spruce top. Very good

(opposite page) View of Mr. Klingler's shop with violins in a cupboard, separated by pieces of felt.

tone and excellent condition.

No. 7 Violin: Conventional throughout except it has a beautifully carved Ram's head and horns on scroll. No maker's label inside. Acquired by Nels Remlin in June, 1957. Good condition.

No. 8 Violin: Odd shaped violin, large model. Lower bouts 8¾" upper bouts 7" wide, 14⅜" long. The nearest style instrument in this particular violin is shown in a picture on Page 115 in Ed Heron Allen's Book. "Violin Making As It was and Is," by George Chanet, Paris 1856. This violin has no C's in the center of the instrument. The lower bout comes to an abrupt corner and forms one half of a C, then tapers to the upper bout. It has rather straight large sound holes. The valute on the scroll is reversed from the conventional violin and turned back rather than forward. Beautiful, curly maple back, ribs and neck. Excellent workmanship, finish and tone. Acquired by Nels Remlin February, 1943.

No. 9 Violin: Conventional, except raised rosettes carved on top and bottom plates at corners at C's. Label inside Lutherie Artisque, F. BARBE, Membre de la Societe Melophile d'Aue 1889. Acquired by Nels Remlin May, 1952. Excellent condition and tone.

No. 10 Violin: Has dove head carved on scroll. Label inside Geo. Batista Gobbrielli fiec in franze 1754. Acquired by Nels Remlin in November, 1939. Excellent condition and tone.

No. 11 Violin: Beautiful carved special head and scroll. At outside corners of C's is a round column, no corners on the ribs, but provided with diamond shaped overlays in place of sharp corners on ribs. Some sort of monogram near neck button of upper bout and beautifully inscribed maple leaf and a bug resembling a cricket in lower bout on back. No maker's name inside. Acquired by Nels Remlin, March, 1943. Excellent condition and tone.

No. 12 Violin: Has beautiful decorative double row purfling on top and back plates. Label inside Joseph Guarnerius Filius Andreae facit, Cremona feit tilulo S. Therefrae 1729. Beautiful curly maple back, ribs and neck. Acquired by E. F. Klingler in 1964.

As an architect, Mr. Klingler built practically every type of building, residences and hospitals. His first public architectural assignment was to build the Polk County jail and sheriff's house. He became a registered architect in 1932 after the Registration Act of 1931, and for sixteen years he served on the Board of Directors of the Wisconsin Architectural Association and Chapter, a branch of the A.I.A. After being Vice-President for two years, he was asked to become President but declined because of Eau Claire's distance from Milwaukee, which was the chief center for architects in the state.

For Mr. Klingler's development from carpenter to violin craftsman, I give his autobiography which is published here for the first time

On October 9, 1887, born to Frank and Frances Klingler at Winona, Minnesota, a son, normal in all respects except upon arrival it was discovered he had two full size teeth to help battle his way through this rough wide world. Some six years later, the Klinglers moved to a 46 acre farm south of Winona, which had absolutely no modern conveniences.

At the age of six, started to attend the rural elementary school located 2 miles from home. The only mode of conveyance was on *foot* through deep snow, since there was no snow removal and the roads from home to school were so located where snow drifts piled up to several feet deep and the thermometer sometimes dropped to as low as 35° below zero.

When the family of four took on a small truck farm, they had very little cash as down payment. Therefore, everybody had to work to make ends meet. Father was a carpenter during the summer and during the winter cut cord wood for the market, which was several miles away. Therefore, he was only home for Sundays. During the summer he worked at carpentry 10 hours each day, including Saturdays.

As to school, my brother, 2 years younger, and I, were lucky to attend some 4 months per year, between doing chores, cutting wood to keep the home fire burning, planting and harvesting and helping mother take the product to town two or three times a week.

In June, 1904, the folks sold our small farm and acquired an 80 acre farm at Amery, Wisconsin. Our family had increased to 6 people. Father wanted to remain at home with the family. As for me, now 15 years old, I had a sixth grade education and had considerable experience in handling and sharpening hand tools since there were no small power tools in those days in our small work shop. My ambition was to become a carpenter and builder. In those days, in small communities, carpenters only worked during the summer months. In the Fall we oiled and packed up our tools and took off for the lumber camp where I worked four winters. During the Fall of 1907–1908, carpenters' work was rather slow towards Fall, so I went threshing wheat in the Dakotas with friends of ours. This usually lasted a couple of months and then back to the sawmill in the lumber camp where I gained much information with various sorts of saws, etc.

In 1909, I purchased a complete encyclopedia, American School of Correspondence on Architecture and Carpentry, and some books on steel square. I did not enroll in the course but studied in my own way in spare moments.

In 1911, I married Emma Volkart of Winona, Minnesota, who, in earlier years, was a neighbor farm girl. We had both attended the same small rural school. Now being married and having worked with various fine carpenters and ending up with a very reliable firm of heavy wood framing contractors, Barret-Threasure of New Richmond, Wisconsin, I learned much in timber framing. In 1911, I also started carpentry work on my own with a crew of four men, my first large project being a timber frame barn 38' x 100', 16' side walls. All points were mortise and tennon, held together with 1" hardwood pegs made by us on the job. In a rather crude way I also prepared my own plans for this job, of which I still have a copy.

In 1913 at the close of the carpentry season, which was November, I came in from the country after a very busy season of 4 large barns, and having no desire to leave my wife and child during the winter to go back to the lumber camp, I did much thinking about getting into something for year-around work. We had difficulty obtaining millwork in the Amery area, and in those days it was necessary to make most of the window and door frames, including much of the trim on the job, with hand carpentry tools. This also happened to be only a few years after the big saw and planing mills moved out of Amery with much scattered lumber left to be manufactured. I conceived the idea of entering into the manufacture of millwork. November 10, 1913, I began work on the erection of a building to house a large planer, matcher, resaws and the other machinery.

By the following fall we began operation. That same year we planed and shipped out 1½ million feet of lumber for a lumberman and other interested people. The following year I entered the field of millwork and row boats, etc. Four years later it became apparent that it was necessary to expand the plant and add a small sawmill and dry kiln to the operation. I also discovered that our site was not large enough to take the expansion, so I picked up the original 36 x 60 two story frame building, including the 16 x 24 engine house, and moved to a new location of 3 acres. We added a sawmill and an addition to house a cabinet shop, boiler room, drier room and lumber storage. We then manufactured a complete line of millwork, church furniture, including some period furniture for the George Washington Antique Furniture Shop at White Bear, Minnesota.

In the meantime I kept up a program of study in architecture during the winter slack months since there wasn't much millwork required in rural communities. The sawmill and manufacturing of lumber dwindled down, snow removal of roads making it impossible to bring in the logs on sleighs, and this was before they knew of trucks for logging.

In 1928 time and conditions changed with the depression coming on which affected millwork plants throughout the country. This was also the beginning of small portable power tools. Most contractors, in order to keep busy, made their own cabinets, etc., and in 1929 we closed down the plant and opened an office to do architecture, having had considerable knowledge in manufacturing all types of millwork, carpentry and buildings, combined with study from my encyclopedias. In 1932, I took an examination and became registered to practice architecture in the State of Wisconsin, up to which time I had designed 29 one room rural schools, 4 two room schools, and one three room school, the Polk County jail, and sheriff's residence, canning factory, etc.

I disposed of the factory and continued with architecture in Amery until 1940 when I moved to Eau Claire, and entered into a partnership with A. H. Hubbard, with offices in the Culver Building. In 1943 we took Wm. T. Gohn, a professional engineer, in as a partner, which partnership ended in August, 1946, when Mr. Hubbard passed away. I took over the architectural practice under the title of E. F. Klingler & Associates which had expanded to 15 people.

In 1952 I received word that the Culver Building was to be torn down, so in the Fall of that year I purchased the Goethel Building located on the west side of the Chippewa River on Grand Avenue in Eau Claire, Wisconsin. I set up the corporation of Emil F. Klingler, Inc., and rebuilt the old store building to the present office. In 1953 we moved our office into the second floor of this present building. Our staff ranged from 14 to 18 people. In 1956 I formed a corporation more adequate to handle the practice which was known as E. F. Klingler & Associates, Inc., with all employees holding at least one share or more of stock. This venture worked out very nicely. We still have 15 to 18 people in our group. Our practice is diversified and consists of the following:

In the early 1940s we did many dairy plants which the government financed during the war. Then came schools, which still predominate, and also many other types of buildings, including a Y.M.C.A., etc., ranging in price up to three million dollars.

Mr. Klingler's last structure was a bomb proof cellar for his home which was constructed after research in Washington, D.C. according to scientific specifications. He keeps his most valuable instruments there.

It is Mr. Klingler's opinion that it is no longer possible for a craftsman to develop in the manner in which he did. The question is, will we ever again have such self-taught craftsmen? Artists, yes; but with the possible exception of stained glass craftsmen, workers developing skills so that they earn their living with their handwork—no. Mr. Klinger is professionally engaged as a violin repairer and dealer, although he still maintains his connection with the architectural firm of E. F. Klingler and Associates, Inc.

V
Ship Model
Craftsmen

SHIP MODEL CRAFTSMEN

Wisconsin had several shipyards in its early days of sailing ships and also counted at least three ship model makers whose productions are of museum caliber and some of which are of interest in Wisconsin maritime history.

Undoubtedly, the most colorful ship model maker was Guy McCracken of Sturgeon Bay, known as Irishman Mac, who retired as a deep sea sailor to the haven of Sturgeon Bay. There he carried on a prolific production of ship models.

He used a great variety of designs extending from caravels to steamships, some historical, others not. The foremost collection of his models was that of Grant Fitch, a Milwaukee banker who maintained a summer home at Fish Creek, Door County, and

(page 76) Square Rigged Ship, modelled by Guy McCracken of Sturgeon Bay, for the collection of the late Grant Fitch, former president of the Marine National Bank, where these type models of Guy McCracken may be seen. Others by him are in the Milwaukee Public Museum. Photo No. 7421–11.

Roman type ship by Guy McCracken. Photo No. 7421–12.

"Constitution," restored twenty or more years ago and moored in Boston Navy Yard. (Recently it sank in a storm.) Model by Guy McCracken. Photo No. 7421–1.

having met Mr. McCracken in 1915, had commissioned about thirty-five of his models. Examples of these can be found at the Marine National Bank of Milwaukee, the Milwaukee Public Museum and the Milwaukee Library Marine Room. He also made models for the Leathem D. Smith Dock Co., Sturgeon Bay; Manitowoc Ship Building Corp.; E. B. Jones, Hancock, Michigan; A. B. Dick Co. of Chicago and many yacht clubs throughout the country.

Guy McCracken was born in Muskegon, Michigan, just after the Civil War and at twenty-one he was first mate on an ocean

Barkentine—built in Sheboygan, in 1867, the owner was Capt. Lyman and was the "Pride of the Lakes."

going windjammer. He sailed the seas for forty years, after which this salty character retired and built his little home in the fresh water port of Sturgeon Bay, Wisconsin. To quote Howard Jamison in a column about Guy McCracken in the Milwaukee Sentinel called "Jaunts with Jamie":

> "With what he liked to call 'my $1.49 equipment—a vegetable knife, a jack knife, a couple of pairs of pliers and my little home-made drill' he carved and whittled all of the parts for his countless accurate models."

He had a peg leg, replacing one bitten off by a shark while being keel-hauled. As a great teller of tales, he relates an experience in the South Seas in an encounter with a hostile islander who chased Irish Mac in a threatening way. The sailor, who was short, stretched a wire between two trees and ran between them whereupon his taller opponent followed furiously and was decapitated.

Fighting ship with ram, by Guy McCracken. Photo No. 7421–6.

Mr. Fred J. Peterson of Peterson Builders, Inc., Sturgeon Bay, said that many of the McCracken models are still about and treasured highly. He still owns one made in 1934 but it was not a replica of a vessel constructed in the Peterson plant. He said that McCracken certainly was a wonderful carver and sailor, and that he knew most of the ships that were sailing the oceans of the world in the latter part of the last century. Guy McCracken had a knack of carving all the sails so that they appeared well filled and authentic.

On a visit to Sturgeon Bay to obtain information about Guy McCracken, I first called upon Clifford Herlache, President of the Bank of Sturgeon Bay. He had been retained as lawyer for the late Mr. McCracken when he had been jailed on a charge of drunkenness, but his client died before the case was concluded.

Shecancoe Riber Gambi. Model by Guy McCracken, Fitch collection.

Caravel by Guy McCracken. Model by Guy McCracken. Photo No. 7411–3.
(preceding double page) Three master barkentine. Photo No. 7411–7.
One of the first "Walk-in-the-Water" steam boats. Model by Guy McCracken. Photo
No. 7421–10.

Mr. Herlache directed me behind the bank to the Nautical Inn where one could see schooners carved by McCracken behind the bar. I saw the row of ship models but neither the inn manager nor the bartender had any information to offer about the craftsman who had made them.

As I left, the bartender said, "I guess he is still living." "No," I told him, "He died in jail, drunk, in 1931." "Well," said the bartender, "I reckon that is as good a place as any to die in if you're drunk."

Schooner rig with square top sail. Photo No. 7411–2.

Mr. Herlache remembered when McCracken hurled a brick through the window of the bank, aiming at the president's office. "Crackpot" was the name most often used in describing this ship model maker, but that was no aspersion on his craftsmanship. Although Guy McCracken's sailing days were spent on the Atlantic Ocean, Sturgeon Bay, where he was employed from time to time with Smith's Tugs, was his last port of call.

(opposite page) Brig with square rig on both masts. Model by Guy McCracken. Photo No. 7421–3.

Brake-rig with power. Photo No. 7411–4.

John Kane, shown with his model of the "Courtland." Photograph by Baynes of Sheboygan.

The ship model maker of Milwaukee is Hans Madsen, whose work is exhibited in the aforementioned Marine Room. His first gift to the Library consisted of nine miniature sailing ships in bottles, but he also gave the Library a model in a glass case, of a four-masted brig called the "Bernie," of the type which sailed the oceans. Another gift was a scale model (one inch per foot) of the 26 foot *Red, White and Blue*, based on an early Currier and Ives lithograph. This ship had sailed July 9, 1866, from New York with Captains Hudson and Fitch aboard alone, and had arrived in Margate, England on August 16. Their motive was to demonstrate the sea worthiness of this new type of lifeboat called "Ingersolls Improved Metallic Life Boat." The model was made of wood, however.

On a farm near Oostburg lives the last schooner captain of the Great Lakes, John Kane, who sailed out of Sheboygan Harbor, and who, in his leisure time, constructed accurate scale models of ships on which he had sailed and one of which he had owned.

Home on Point of Land, West of Sturgeon Bay, owned by Guy McCracken, but later remodeled.

The "Rosa Belle," owned and modeled by John Kane, in 1969, the last surviving schooner captain on the lakes.

(opposite page) The "Courtland" sailing out of Sheboygan and partly owned by John Kane's father. Model by John Kane according to scale. Photograph by Gerhard Bakker.

Three-master, named the "Bernie," modeled by Hans C. Madsen, now in the Marine Room of the Milwaukee Public Library.

Kane was born in Sheboygan in 1884 and lived with his daughter's family on the Wilson-Lima Road in Sheboygan County. His schooling lasted through the first year of high school. He started sailing at the age of eighteen, first with his father and with his mother who was the cook. He is now a "landlubber," but his whole career was based on ships; first sailing schooners; then in both World Wars working at the Manitowoc Shipyards on submarines. He has always pursued his hobby of making scale models of the sailing vessels which he had known. These included his own *Rosa Belle*, the *Courtland* on which his father sailed, and the *Lottie Cooper* of the Groh Fleet.

John Kane's memory is very sharp and he loves to talk about sailing on the Great Lakes. He last sailed in 1917, but by that time he had sailed all over Lake Michigan on ships carrying lumber, pine and hardwood, slabs, and bark for tanneries. One of his most vivid memories was a story his father told him of a wreck on Lake Huron. I quote from a letter he wrote to me about the ship on which his father had sailed:

> Thinking you would like to hear some of the Courtland's history, she was built at the Johnson Shipyard in Sheboygan in 1867 and was considered one of the finest ships on the lakes. My father shipped in her in the spring of 1868, and while on her way to Buffalo with a cargo of grain, she was in collision with the passenger steamship, *Morning Star*. This happened in a dense fog on Lake Erie five miles off Cleveland. Both ships sank with a loss of 250 lives. My father, although badly injured, was rescued the next morning after clinging to a piece of the cabin for five hours. This happened on the 20th of June, 1868, on his 21st birthday. The Courtland was the pride of the A. P. Lyman fleet of seven schooners sailing from Sheboygan.

All lake vessels entering Sheboygan Port were tied up at the Kirkland and Curtis Pier from which all merchandise consigned to merchants at Fond du Lac, Oshkosh, and other points, were hauled away by teams over the plank road to their respective destinations.

Early view of Sheboygan Harbor, showing fishing boats, schooner, Riebolt and Walters Dry Dock, Cocker Chair Company, with grain elevator on right.

Painting of a schooner by E. Groh, 1889, the "Sardinia," of the Groh Fleet. Flag shows a chair and a sofa as indication of Sheboygan's chief products. From the collection of Frank C. Jacobson.

Sheboygan Harbor was developed for schooners seeking shelter from storms, shipwrecks and fires. From 1852 to 1871, there had been expended on the harbor by the federal government $105,488.91, by the county $42,796.41, and by the city $26,700.00. The North and South Piers on which were built privately owned warehouses. Later, however, they were government controlled.* In 1863 over fifty sailing vessels and four steamers were sighted in the harbor. Seventeen were owned in Sheboygan and later seven were lost. Thirty schooners could be seen at one time and fifty laid up. Steamboats could not compete at first, but schooners quit in 1916. The *Lady Elgin* used to stop in Sheboygan on her way to Chicago from Buffalo.

In those days the schooners unloaded coal in hogsheads by means of pulleys in the rigging which was powered by a horse. Commodities handled were cord wood, wheat, flour, shingles, barrels, hubs, fish, potash, and salt from Buffalo.

John Kane never worked for the Groh Fleet, but remembers it well. On its roster were the *Lottie Cooper, Evening Star, Jos. Duvall, Sardinia* and the *L. E. Raesser*. These schooners carried a Sheboygan flag showing a couch and a chair as emblems of the city's chief manufacturers.

John Kane made his meticulously rigged models in his leisure time. Among them was the *Laura May,* a two master with sails which at first had cloth and later aluminum sails, the *Courtland,* the *Lottie Cooper,* and his own *Rosa Belle.* John Kane used wire for rigging on some of his models, with masts and hulls of wood.

F. Groh, son of the fleet founder, made water colors of all of the Groh Fleet. They can be viewed in the Office of Frank Jacobson in Sheboygan. The water color of the *Sardinia* is shown here.

Kane's own *Rosa Belle* was built in 1863 in Milwaukee and

* Reference: Historic Sheboygan County by Gustave William Buchen. Printed 1944.

was lost in 1921 near that city when an explosion caused the loss of twelve lives. Today the remains of the Rosa Belle lie on the sand near the Racine Yacht Club.

One hundred years ago the *Toledo* went down a little south of Port Washington. On John Kane's advice scuba divers went down and found a box of six axe heads and three jackknives. He

"Alice of Kenosha" was a typical three masted schooner with a raffee on the foremast. It was launched about 1890 and was about 125 feet long. The owners were N. R. Allen and Sons, and Edward Thiers. For many years she carried tan bark from Green River (now Charlevoix), Michigan, to the tannery at Kenosha. The model is the work of Capt. John S. Rice, and is now at the Milwaukee Yacht Club, of which he was a long time member.

The "Quaviver" is an auxiliary ketch whose owner and master is Capt. Louis Quarles of Milwaukee. It was built by the Central Shipyard Co., of Long Island, New York, and was launched June 17, 1936, and is 46 feet long. The model was made in 1954 by Captain John Rice.

told me that the *Phoenix*, which burned to the water level five miles out of Sheboygan in 1847 and was towed in and covered with sand, lies under the present auditorium near Sheboygan Harbor.

Steamboats couldn't compete at first, but after the schooners, the steamers *"Troy"* and *"Queen City"* plied between Sheboygan and other ports; the *"Clement"* between Chicago and Sheboygan. Those were the days of skating parties and bratwurst roasts on the

The Atlantic, three masted schooner, was owned by Robert A. Uihlein and Erwin C. Uihlein, both at times having been presidents of the Jos. Schlitz Brewing Co. of Milwaukee. It was built by the Bethlehem Ship Building Co., at Sparrows' Point, Maryland in 1927. It was designed by Gielow, Inc., New York City and carried a Krupp diesel engine. It had been bought by the Uihleins in 1932 and its length was 120 feet.

For many years it was moored north of the Cherry Street Bridge on the Milwaukee River and had accommodations for fourteen people as guests and a crew of twelve.

In World War I, Erwin Uihlein served as commandant of a naval gun plant in Bedford, Ohio, and in World War II he served the coast guard as Lieutenant Commander of the U.S.S. Hawk. Robert Uihlein served as state chairman of the Wis. Citizen's Committee for Naval Relief in 1942.

The Atlantic was commissioned in World War II by the coast guard for submarine detection and was credited with "assists" in two sub kills. It then carried eleven guns. After the war the ship was given by the owners to Texas A. & M. Research Foundation for service as a floating marine laboratory and was so equipped as a "Class A" weather station for ships in the Gulf of Mexico.

Gerhardt Bakker photographer.

(opposite page) Model of Atlantic by? Christianson.

ice in the middle of winter.

A recent visit to the ship model section of the Smithsonian Institution in Washington, D.C., disclosed no model of a ship built in a Wisconsin shipyard bordering on Lake Michigan.

Shipbuilding began in Manitowoc in 1847 with the building of the schooner *"Citizen"* by Captain Joseph Edwards. Several companies build wooden ships, but all of these early ones passed out of existence except The Burger Boat Company, Inc., which was later purchased by Manitowoc Drydock Co. (The drydock came from Chicago). The Manitowoc Shipyards in 1901 had built 125 sailing vessels, 40 steamboats, 35 tugs and divers small craft. In the 1920s-30s, they built fruit carriers, dredges, tugs, and the self-unloader *"Charles C. West."* In the 1930s-40s the speed crane was developed, the tanker *"Red Crown"* and the carferry *"City of Midland"* were built. In 1940, 28 submarines were ordered, and in 1942 landing craft and tankers. In the years since World War II the Manitowoc Ship Building Co. concerned itself with building large commercial lake freighters. Two products were the 639 foot self-unloading *"J. Boland"* built in 1953 and the *"Edward L. Ryerson,"* a 730 foot ore carrier which, when built in 1960, was the largest ever seen on the Great Lakes. The Manitowoc Ship Building Co. survives, but since World War II its activities have been diversified to the extent that in the 1965 Great Lakes *Red Book* no ship was listed by that company.

Other cities have had shipyards or repair stations as the one on Jones Island, Milwaukee, as well as the Froemming yards up the Kinnickinnic River; in Sturgeon Bay was the Christy Corporation and Peterson Builders, Inc.; in Superior, the Fraser Shipyards, Inc.; in Marinette, the Kargard Co. and The Marinette Marine Corporation which did building and repair.

When you consider the giant ore boat *"Ryerson"* plying the route from Chicago to Superior (I have taken two trips on the Inland Steel ships), it is historically interesting to consider that my friend John Kane once captained a schooner on the same lake and has produced accurate models of the ships on which he sailed.

Unrelated but interesting information about a model owned by
Robert S. Stevenson of Elm Grove, Wisconsin.

These bone models belonged to the category of prisoner-of-war models, made during the Napoleonic Wars by French prisoners in England. Between the years 1798 and 1815, many French ships were taken by the English. The crews were thrown into prison, especially at Dartmouth, and at other places such as Rochester Castle, Norman-Cross, Perth, and elsewhere. Often they were kept in prison on decommissioned war ships, so-called hulks, especially at Portsmouth, Devonport, and Chatham.

Amongst them were ivory carvers from Dieppe and West Africa. Although the bulk of these prisoners was made up of Frenchmen, there were also many Spanish and Dutch among them. When in 1801 the English fleet bombarded Copenhagen, they captured many Danish ships, and Danish sailors began to share the fate of Napoleon's sailors. In the War of 1812, American sailors started to swell the ranks of the prisoners.

These prisoners were a motley crowd. However, the industrious among them soon began to produce small articles, as souvenirs, to be bartered for food and tobacco. In the course of time

Palm and needles used by sailors in mending sail. From the collection of Frank C. Jacobson, Sheboygan.

the work became organized and work-teams were formed. They made tobacco-boxes, canes, figurines, and the like, but ship models became the most favored objects, because they brought the highest prices.

FRIGATE, BUILDING AT LYONS
BUILT AT FRANCE PRESENTED FROM THE NAPOLEONIC WARS
WAS A CAPTIVE IN ENGLAND 1792-1815
ERECT A COUNCIL OF THE GOVERNMENT AND AUTHORITIES ACTING
IN THE SAME ARGUMENT INCLUDED DURING THE YEAR 1757-1758
IN THE YEAR 1758

These models were often marvels of craftsmanship, especially so in view of the lack of the customary and necessary tools. A knife was often the only instrument available. If possible, other tools were made of scraps of metal, old nails, and whatever materials could be found. Sewing needles were used for drills to bore holes for rivets. Sometimes the guards connived with the prisoners, supplying badly needed tools since they were interested in obtaining such models and selling them to visitors and local curio dealers. The material for the hull, masts, and spars consisted mostly of beef bones, collected from meals. But ivory, wood, whale bone, and sometimes metal, were also used. Although guns were usually made of brass or bone, in some instances they were made of gold, just as were the bands around the masts, and other small items.

Looking at such masterpieces now, one marvels at the patience and skill it took to make them. But time was of no account to the prisoners. In the case of the smaller models, with the minutest detailed work and carving, it is inconceivable that the tiny blocks or eyebolts, the size of a pinhead, could have been made without the use of a magnifying glass.

Just as in a real ship, the frames of the models were mostly made of wood, to which planks were correctly and neatly fitted, with tiny rivets, made of copper, silver or gold. Bone cannot be bent like wood, therefore the curved plank had to be whittled, although the builders probably took advantage of natural bends and curves. The rigging was usually made of thread; however, in smaller models, horsehair was often used for the standing rigging, and human hair for the running gear, because it was easily available.

Prisoner-of-war models are usually very correct in their proportions, although not true scale models, because the prisoners did not have actual plans at their disposal. They had to rely on their knowledge of ships and their memory.

(page 102) Model made of ivory by prisoners, etc., from the collection of Robert Stevenson.

VI
Wesley W. Jung
and his
Carriage Collection

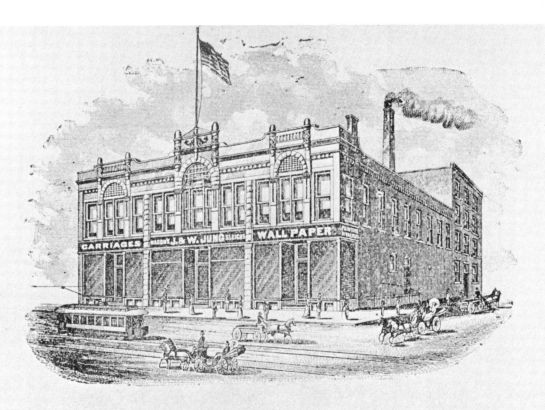

J. & W. JUNG,

Fabrikanten von

Wagen, Kutschen und Schlitten

und Händler in

Maler und Dekorateure.

**Farben, Oelen,
Plate= u. Fensterglas,
Tapeten re.,**

SHEBOYGAN, WIS.

Dieses Geschäft wurde im Jahre 1855 von Herrn Jacob Jung Sr. gegründet und stand dasselbe bis zum Jahre 1890 unter seiner Leitung. In genanntem Jahre übertrug er das Geschäft käuflich an seine zwei ältesten Söhne, Jacob Jung Jr. und Wm. Jung. Herr Jacob Jung Sr. befaßte sich nur mit der Fabrikation von Wagen und Kutschen, während die Söhne auch ein Maler= und Dekorations=Departement, sowie eine umfangreiche Tapetenhandlung einführten. Ferner führen J. & W. Jung Farben, Öle, Fensterglas etc. in großer Auswahl.

Das Wagen= und Kutschen=Departement steht unter Leitung von Jacob Jung Jr., während Wm. Jung dem Maler und Dekorations= Departement vorsteht.

WESLEY W. JUNG
AND HIS
CARRIAGE COLLECTION

Wesley W. Jung at work ornamenting the child's chariot wheels.

Of the many crafts practised in Wisconsin, one of the most exacting was carriage and wagon making. It entailed a knowledge of wood working, blacksmithing or ironing, painting and varnishing, upholstering or trimming and striping, besides the art of designing the various wagons, carriages, sleighs, fire wagons, lumber wagons, and mail carts desired by the customer. Since these conveyances have all been superseded by gasoline burning trucks and cars, carriage making has become a lost art. The restoration by Wesley W. Jung of Sheboygan, Wisconsin of his collection, around 125 wagons and carriages, demonstrates a decided feat of craftsmanship.

(page 106) Building where Wesley Jung's father was sent by his father to learn the wagonmaking trade at about 1879.

Mr. Jung acquired his knowledge of the many necessary skills by working in the J. & W. Jung Co., a wagon works which Jacob Jr. and William Jung had purchased from their father, the original Jacob Jung, in 1887. The founder, who was born in Noettingen in the Grand Duchy of Baden, Germany, in 1831, came to Sheboygan as a young immigrant wheelwright in 1854 and found employment with the Brother and Jones Wagon Works. He and a partner, in a settlement for unpaid wages, later became owners of that company.

(pagés 108 and 109) A corner in Wesley W. Jung's shop, Sheboygan, Wisconsin, showing men readying vehicles for the new Jung Carriage Museum at Greenbush, Wisconsin.

Wesley Jung was born in 1899. When he completed high school in 1916 at the age of 16, and had been working fourteen months in the paint, wood and blacksmithing shops of the Jung Carriage Company, he was advised by his father since the carriage trade was on a marked decline, to go to the University and enter a professional field which would insure his future. He attended Ripon College and the University of Wisconsin until 1920, and since 1929 has headed an accounting firm in Sheboygan, Jung, Dippold and Cooper.

Following is a quotation from Wisconsin's "Then and Now," published by the State Historical Society of Wisconsin, November 1965:

"About 1898, the proprietor of a traveling dog and pony show came to Mr. Jung's father and asked him to design and build a child-sized police patrol wagon for use in his show. He agreed to do so, and when he completed the drawing, he was so intrigued that he changed the order to his supplier to call for two sets of hubs instead of one. It had occurred to him that his children ought to have one also. For years, Mr. Wesley Jung dreamed that he would find the twin. Then, in 1960, he was pictured in an article in the Sheboygan Press with his own child-sized patrol wagon. The next day, he received a startling telephone call from Mr. Albert Laun of Kiel. Mr. Laun said, 'I want you to

know that I have one exactly like it, which still carries the Jung Carriage Company Name Plate.' The Laun wagon was acquired by Mr. Jung for his collection, and restored to factory newness; however, the present gold leaf lettering is the original. It had lasted for 67 years."

It was about 1939 that Mr. Jung became fascinated with the idea of collecting and restoring examples of old wagons and carriages from the family factory.

The Wesley Jung Collection started with a small patrol wagon made by his father for his children which was also used by Wesley Jung's children. It is still in use and in perfect condition but has worn out 4 sets of rubber tires. From far and wide throughout Sheboygan County, by purchase or gift, different types of vehicles have been accumulated and painstakingly restored by

The original Jung label found on a heavy snow wagon after the dark green paint job, done by a previous owner, was removed.

Wesley Jung himself with the aid of a Sheboygan blacksmith, Emil Reinbacher. Mr. Jung has provided the necessary knowledge and did the painting and striping himself with steady hand. The trimming of the carriages has been done by Gordon Thill. There was much technical knowledge necessary for the making of wagons and especially of carriages. Specialists developed; such as wheelwrights who used hickory wood and spokes. Rural blacksmiths still made wheels, fitting and shaping the spokes, steaming and bending the fellies or rims, for the massive rim bender. "Ironing them off" means fitting on the heavy iron tires. Most of the wheels now are made for the circus wagons at Baraboo.

Hub makers used elm and the panels were of white oak. Blacksmiths made the fifth wheels or turntables under the driver's seats and other metal workers furnished the fine brass work. There were tire setters, and even today in Sheboygan a grease specialist supplies axle grease to the Sturbridge Village Museum for its carriage collection. The cloth for trimming had to be specially sponged so as not to shrink in the rain. There were appropriate varnishes. (One supply company in 1844, Minet & Company of Delawanna, N.J. advertised *Coach and Carriages and Japans*.) Patent leather was made by a heat treatment with black varnish. At the time of World War II none was made, and Wesley Jung had to wait for the war to end to get the proper patent leather for his buck boards (with whip socket at the side). Great care had to be taken to prevent dust from falling onto the fresh varnishes.

There was more variety of design in the carriage industry than in the automobile industry. American carriages were lighter than the English which were built to ride heavily. The buggy and the Rockaway Coupe were typical American designs. The knowledge of carriage making is almost extinct today, but in Wesley Jung and his auxiliary craftsmen it still lives. In other states there are a few manufacturers; such as the Frizzell Coach and Wheel Works in Oklahoma City which makes American coaches; Arkla at Emmet, Arkansas, and Hoopes Bros., at Westchester, Pennsylvania. The authentic reproductions of the early American colonial horse drawn vehicles at Williamsburg, Virginia, were designed from painstaking research by Lt. Colonel Paul H. Downing.

Brewster of Broome Street, New York, when carriage making was at its height, won, in its carriage department in the International Exposition held in Paris in 1878, a Gold Medal for the whole exhibit, and the President of France presented Henry Brewster with the Legion of Honor.

Double end steering hook and ladder wagon with front wheel braking system. Built by Jung about 1890 for the city of Sheboygan, Wisconsin.

113

Only a handful remains of the 28,382 carriage and wagon makers and the 10,316 dealers in the United States. Designs of carriages may be found in the publication of the Carriage Association started in this country in 1961. It was called The *Coachman's Horn* and in 1963 *The Carriage Journal*. Wesley Jung helped organize the association and was the treasurer from 1960 to 1965.

No. 45, Silsby double rotary turbine steam fire engine (pumper). The engine is in perfect working order.

Work on circus wagons under Chappie Fox at Baraboo, Wisconsin, is revived through the inauguration in Milwaukee on July 4, 1963, the first horse drawn circus parade in forty years, under the auspices of the Joseph Schlitz Brewing Company. The wagons used were from the Baraboo collection in the Circus Museum of

Lead carriage in the 1966 Schlitz Fourth of July Parade with Mr. and Mrs. Robert A. Uihlein, Jr., aboard, using Wesley W. Jung's landau. Driver is William Royer of Springfield, Illinois. This aristocratic vehicle has been the lead carriage in many parades and ceremonies carrying dignitaries and officials (see following double page).

the State Historical Society, drawn by 300 horses which came from around Wisconsin, Illinois and Iowa. The Governor rode with his wife in Wesley Jung's landau.

In 1958 for the American Legion Exhibit of fifty vehicles from his "101" collection, Wesley Jung engaged Arthur Heller, a Lindeman Circus professional with many years of calliope playing, to play his calliope. One number he played was a Ringling Bros. favorite, "Entry of the Gladiators." Mr. Jung's circus wagon was built by John H. Richardson and his brother of Sheboygan Falls. The compressed air calliope is from the old Seils-Sterling circus which once wintered in Sheboygan. In 1952 Cleaver Brooks

Company acquired the "Great America" wagon and the steam calliope mounted on her.

Of the items in the collection, 60% were made in Sheboygan by the Jung Carriage Company. The collection was started by Wesley Jung with the idea of preserving specimens put out by that company. Other carriage collections are at Stony Brook, Long Island, the Shelbourne Museum of the J. Watson Webbs in Vermont, the Smithsonian Institute in Washington, and the Henry Ford Museum at Dearborn, Michigan.

Canopy-top surrey This is the surrey used in the Sheboygan Community Players production of "Oklahoma," at North Side High School, in 1957. (NOTE: The late world famous architect, Frank Lloyd Wright, added substantial historical value by sending a truck for it so that he could ride in this surrey heading the Spring Green Centennial Parade June 30, 1957. His truck made four trips of 165 miles each, or a total of 660 miles, including vehicle return trips, to make the fifteen-minute ride possible.) (Jung's Sheboygan Collection No. 85.)

(opposite page) Circus Calliope Wagon in the 1953 Centennial Parade, Sheboygan. The large department store in the background, still owned by the Jung's, but leased to Interstate, was developed as the carriage and wagon business declined.

(pages 120 & 121) Plymouth Hook, Ladder and Hose Reel. (Jung's Sheboygan Collection No. 14.)

No. 84, grocery delivery wagon made by Jacob Jung for the Neumeister Grocery. Now in the Jung Museum at Greenbush.

The future of the Jung collection of horse-drawn vehicles seemed assured when, on Wednesday, June 26, 1963, the State Assembly concurred in a Senate approved bill establishing a Wesley W. Jung Carriage Museum at Wade House State Park at Greenbush. At first the construction of a fitting building to house the collection of 120 vehicles would be assumed by the State Historical Society which would solicit private donations. Governor Reynolds signed that bill, but it was not until July 10, 1967 that ground was broken. The Milwaukee Journal of May 9, 1967, reported that;

> The State building commission Monday approved the construction of a carriage museum at the Old Wade House State Park in Greenbush (Sheboygan County).
>
> The museum which will house a collection of more than 100 hand and horse drawn vehicles will cost $120,000 with the state providing $70,000 and Sheboygan County the remaining $50,000.
>
> The museum was authorized by the 1965 legislature. It will be named the Wesley W. Jung Carriage Museum, after the donor of the vehicles. They are valued at more than $500,000. The State Historical Society of Wisconsin said

(opposite page) No. 69, Armour Wood Tank Sprinkler Wagon. Note the Armour emblem in gold leaf, a splendid restoration, which is now in the Jung Carriage Museum.

At left, No. 69, a side view.

the museum "should greatly increase the annual visitor statistics for the site" and enhance its value.

A coach from the Jung collection (an original Fred Pabst item) now carries passengers on trips about Greenbush for patrons of the Wade House Tours. With the addition of this distinguished collection of wagons and carriages, Wade House State Park and its old stage-coach Inn, will attract visitors from all over our country and enhance this important site of the State Historical Society.

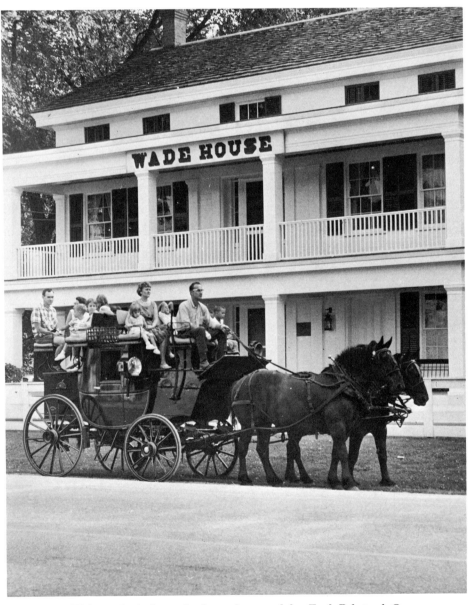

Park Drag. This steel tired coach, formerly owned by Fred Pabst of Oconomowoc, Wisconsin. It is now used on the grounds of the Wade House in Greenbush, Wisconsin, to take visitors on rides (on Tuesdays). This was a gift to Wesley Jung from the family of Curt Joa of Sheboygan Falls. It was built by C. P. Kimball and Co., of Chicago.

Main Street Livery—a twelve passenger curtain omnibus built by J. and W. Jung, Sheboygan, Wisconsin, about 1885. It is owned by Mrs. Lansing Lamont, Mr. Jung's daughter, and was acquired by Mr. Jung on September 12, 1945, from Louis Stark, who, for many years, operated a resort hotel at Crystal Lake.

No. 88, Three Horse Brewery Wagon. This valuable and unique specimen was used by and acquired from the KURTH BREWERY at COLUMBUS, Wisconsin. "Kingsbury" paid for the paint job in exchange for permission to use it in a Sheboygan "Bratwurst Day" parade where it is shown above. William NAJACHT Sr. is driving his Belgian sorrels 3 abreast.

The small photograph is intended to show students how the draft is evenly distributed by one horse hitched to the long end of the evener while an additional evener for the other 2 is attached to the short end.

This Studebaker wide track stake truck has also been reequiped by Mr. Jung for 2 horse use with one pole. In the smaller picture you can see the 2 sockets for 2 poles for a 3 horse hitch.

No. 24, Circus Calliope Wagon. The complete story of this wagon, written by John H. Richardson of Sheboygan Falls, is under plexiglass attached to one of the rear door panels, inside. Mr. Jung's initial investment was $25.00. A later offer of $25,000.00 had to be refused because of Mr. Jung's determination to see this amazing wagon get into the museum as a tribute to his many friends who pitched in to help him make his dream of a circus calliope wagon come true.

It weighs 5 tons, has 5 inch square steel axles and huge wood hub wheels that are among the largest in existence. It has appeared in many parades in Wisconsin and never failed to create excitement.

No. 3, Herzog Heavy Meat Wagon. This vehicle was designed, built and used to haul the carcasses of beef, veal, pork and mutton from Herzog's slaughter house to Sheboygan retail meat markets. In the opinion of Col. Downing, editor of the Carriage Journal, Mr. Jung made a perfect restoration. It has been restored to the identical condition when it was first used by Mr. Herzog.

The original purchase order dated 9-24-04, with completed specifications, is still in Mr. Jung's files. The cost $135.00 complete.

As additional testimony to Mr. Jung's outstanding craftsmanship and restoration ability, there stands next to this wagon in the museum, a beautiful winter version with box mounted on graceful bob runners. These mates and a light 2 wheeled cart for retail delivery of meat to the housewife, stand together to tell a story at the Wesley W. Jung Carriage Museum in Wade House State Park at Greenbush, Sheboygan County.

No. 77, Four Passenger Bob Sleigh. This picture shows Mr. and Mrs. WESLEY W. JUNG and the author in the center, aboard sleighs made by Mr. Jung's grandfather. The one in front is an 1860 model and illustrates the early art of bending solid wood for the graceful dash boards. The vehicles shown are in process of restoration.

Amazingly at this moment there are 5 of the stout but light and easy running 1860 models still known to exist.

Made long before the development of plywood, the solid wood bent dash board are still free of cracks. Jung customers got their money's worth.

(opposite page, center) No. 11, Child's Push Sleigh with interior trim.
This is another splendid example of the art of bending solid wood for dash board and molded side panels.
A Jung product of 1890 for the family of Henry Nagel, Sheboygan.
Beautifully it stands as a museum piece in the Wesley W. Jung Carriage Museum.

(opposite page, bottom) No. 12, Child Size Push Sleigh. This picture was taken in Washington, D.C. where this beauty was used by children of the Lansing Lamont family for several years. Mrs. Lansing Lamont, nee Ada Jung, Mr. Jung's daughter, once wrote. "Your child's sleigh always brings forth many oohs and ahs. Little Tommy was bundled up and enjoying a good hours long ride this afternoon. He put his head back, looked up at the clouds, and let the snow pelt against his face. He could not have had a better time. If and when I have to return this little gem I am tempted to have it copied so all my grandchildren can have as good a time as Tom and Ginny have had."

No. 65, Self-Unloader Coal Wagon. This rare item was appraised July 5, 1968 at $4,000.00. It is the only one left of the hundreds of thousands of coal wagons which at one time before World War I (1914–1918) brought fuel to the homes, stores, schools and factories of America. It was very well built for hard use by STREICH of Oshkosh, Wisconsin and is now a museum piece. It is equipped for either a 2 or 3 horse hitch. The front can be raised by cranking so coal will readily flow out the rear. It was acquired from the Van Der Meere Coal Company of Chicago.

No. 23, Extension Top Phaeton. Made in 1905 by the Jung Carriage Company for lumberman E. E. Pantzer, it is equipped with full eleptic springs, and rubber tires that provide its occupants with an unbelievably smooth ride. The top folds back like a modern automobile convertible but in case of bad weather can be quickly raised. It stands equipped with a complete set of side curtains to protect its occupants. The picture shows the phaeton after restoration by Mr. Jung. The original construction and recent restoration are illustrations of master craftsmanship.

No. 25, Fire Hose Wagon, before restoration. Preparing to pick up the J. & W. J. built fire hose wagon at Gillett, are William Najacht Jr., Rudy Eirich, Fred Schneekloth and William Najacht. What a colossal restoration job lies ahead. Is any more proof needed of Wes Jung's craftsmanship than is shown by the fire wagon after restoration?

No. 25, Fire Hose Wagon, After Restoration. This masterpiece of design and construction by J. & W. Jung about 1890 is the subject of much admiration. America's foremost builder of horsedrawn vehicles in miniature, Ivan L. Collins, featured in LIFE a few years ago, has duplicated this beauty in 1/8 scale for permanent display in the ERB Memorial Building, University of Oregon at Eugene. For exact reproduction in miniature, Mr. Collins called for and was provided with countless measurements and specifications by Mr. Jung as well as 60 close up professional photographs from end to end, as well as sides, top and bottom. The pictures show every detail of the platform spring suspension system. No bracket, clip, shackle clevis or fifth wheel detail was overlooked by Collins who also traveled to Sheboygan, Wisconsin in 1969 to make a personal inspection.

No. 85, Canopy Top Surrey. This is the type of surrey that was featured so prominently in the stage play and movie "*OKLAHOMA*" where it was called the "SURREY WITH THE FRINGE ON TOP." Carriage builders called them "Canopy Top Surreys." The picture shows our craftsman, Wesley W. Jung with his daughter-in-law Barbara and grandchildren. This vehicle was a "basket case" when found but was patiently restored. "Its wheels are yellow, the upholstery's* brown, the dashboard's genuine leather." "It is complete with "2 bright side lights.

*Carriage men say TRIM, never upholstery, a furniture term.

No. 50, Racing Sulky. This early American racing sulky is quite a contrast to the modern low wire wheeled racing sulkies. This museum piece has large and light but stout staggered spoke wood hub wheels with a fascinating brass ferrule on one spoke that is intended to provide the rider with the ability to accurately measure a given distance such as a quarter, half or full mile by counting the necessary number of revolutions at a walk.

This sulky was acquired in pieces from Ralph De Smith, Sheboygan Falls. Anyone truly interested in the fine art of high grade carriage restoration work should give this item careful study.

No. 53, "Velvet Tobacco Wagon. Boldly and beautifully proclaiming "Velvet, The Smoothest Tobacco for Smoking" this light but strongly built delivery wagon was built for Herman Schuelke, tobacconist and former Sheboygan mayor by J. and W. Jung about 1900. It's bevel edged plate glass side windows and special paint job made it outstanding in the days before the automobile. Mr. and Mrs. George Wellhoefer made Wesley W. Jung a gift of this valuable and historic gem knowing full well it could not get into more appreciative hands and would hopefully someday go to his intended museum which has since become a fact.

No. 22, William Braasch Rockaway. This dignified rubber tired coupe has also been restored in the Jung manner. The glass is new beveled edge plate glass. The lamps are in working order and the dark board is genuine patent leather. It was used for many years by the late William Braasch, head of the Sheboygan Chair Company, once one of Wisconsin's most important industries.

No. 66, Convertible Top Buggy. An excellent specimen of a J. & W. Jung built top buggy. It is rubber tired for a smooth quiet ride with CONCORD type side springs for the ultimate in comfort. This sporty convertible, now in the musuem, was acquired from Max Heffernan of Ripon, Wisconsin.

No. 76, Roof Seat Omnibus. Here is one of the most valuable items in the famous Jung collection. The interior is trimmed expertly with $14.00 per yard imported Bedford Cord fabric by Gordon Thill under Mr. Jung's exacting scrutiny. It was acquired from the late Frank Lloyd Wright and expensively and painstakingly rebuilt. Joe Bartel, Ralph Bender and Jake Clicquenoi gave their best talents also to make this rare gem a worthwhile subject for close study. New rubber tires of course were installed in place of the old.

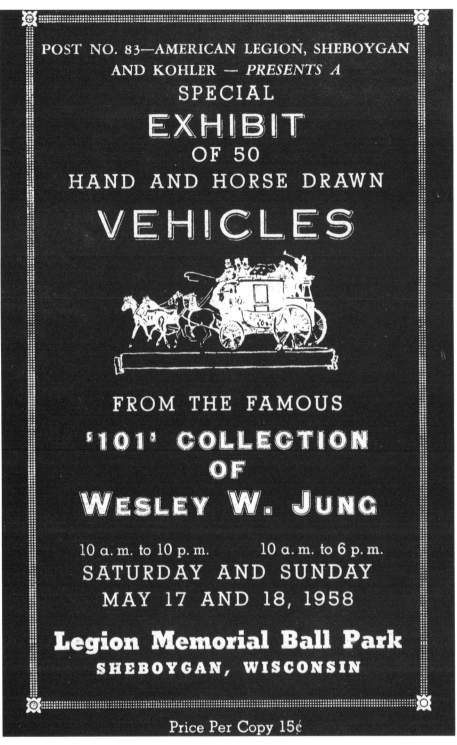

POST NO. 83—AMERICAN LEGION, SHEBOYGAN
AND KOHLER — *PRESENTS A*
SPECIAL
EXHIBIT
OF 50
HAND AND HORSE DRAWN
VEHICLES

FROM THE FAMOUS
'101' COLLECTION
OF
WESLEY W. JUNG

10 a.m. to 10 p.m.   10 a.m. to 6 p.m.
SATURDAY AND SUNDAY
MAY 17 AND 18, 1958

Legion Memorial Ball Park
SHEBOYGAN, WISCONSIN

Price Per Copy 15¢

So highly regarded is Mr. Jung's collection and craftsmanship, that both houses of the Wisconsin Legislature, the Senate and Assembly, voted in 1963 without a single dissent to provide a special museum in his honor.

VEHICLE
NUMBER

1 Wesley's 1st Ward Child Size Police Patrol Wagon
2 Yellow Child Size Coasting Bob
3 Herzog Heavy Meat Wagon
4 Child Size Hand Drawn Flat Bed Hauling Bob
5 Child Size Hauling Bob Sled
6 Heavy Lumber Wagon
7 Main Street Livery Carry-All, Curtain Omnibus
8 1 Horse Light Dray Wagon
9 Child's Size Coasting Bob
10 Pull Type Girl's Coasting Sled
11 Child Size Portland Style Push Sleigh
12 White Body Mint Green Ornamented Child's Push Sleigh
13 Auto Seat End Spring Top Buggy
14 Plymouth, Wisconsin Hand Drawn Hook and Ladder Wagon

15 Plymouth, Wisconsin Hand Drawn Hose Reel
16 4 Horse, 10 Passenger—Vis-A-Vis "Russian" Sleigh
17 4 Horse "Pabst" Park Drag
18 4 Passenger, 2 Seated Bob Sleigh
19 3 Spring Portland Cutter with Doors
20 J & W Jung Co. Delivery Bob Sled
21 J & W Jung Co. Open Delivery Wagon "No. 14"
22 William Braasch's Cut-Under Coupe Rockaway
23 Extension Top Phaeton
24 Circus Calliope Wagon
25 Gillette, Wisconsin Fire Department Hose Wagon
26 Rubber Tired Concord Runabout
27 "Concord" Side Spring Top Buggy
28 Light Portland Cutter
29 Geo. W. F. Herzog 3 Spring Handy Wagon
30 Geo. W. F. Herzog Heavy Meat Delivery Bob Sled
31 "Edna J" Child Size Coasting Bob
32 Mail Carrier's Cutter
33 Main Carrier's Cutter
34 Rubber Tired Spindle Seat End Spring Runabout or No-Top Road Wagon
35 No Doors, No Springs, Portland Cutter
36 3 Spring Portland Cutter
37 Cut-Under Basket Seat Phaeton
38 Child Size "Russian Druschka" or Victoria
39 Child Size Coaster or Express Wagon
40 Prairie Schooner Covered Wagon
41 Swell Body Cutter
42 Ladies Queen Side Basket Phaeton
43 2 Passenger Rubber Tired Brougham
44 5 Glass Landau
45 Silsby Double Rotary Steam Turbine Pumper
46 Oblong Box Steel Tired Top Buggy
47 No Top Steel Tired Runabout or Road Wagon
48 Foeste 2 Passenger Portland Cutter
49 Plymouth Hand Drawn Chemical Fire Wagon
50 Wood Wheel Staggered Spoke Racing Sulky
51 Knocke Meat Market 2 Wheel Delivery Car
52 Elkhart Lake, Wisconsin Hook & Ladder Wagon
53 "Velvet" Tobacco Wagon

54 Elkhart Lake, Wisconsin Hand Drawn Hose Reel
55 Oblong Steel Tired Top Buggy
56 Governess Cart
57 Jimmy, Johnny, Jennifer Jung Coasting Bob
58 Farm Wagon with Hay Rack
59 Dillingham Factory Wood Dump Wagon
60 A. L. & C. H. Laun Child Size Police Wagon
61 4 Passenger 2 seated High Grade De Luxe Bob Sleigh
62 Side Spring Portland Cutter with Doors
63 Plain, no springs, no doors, Portland Cutter
64 Swell Body Cutter
65 3 Horse Self-Unloader Coal Wagon
66 "Concord" Side-spring Rubber-tired Top Buggy
67 Jump Seat Cutter
68 Oblong Box Rubber-tired Spindle Seat Runabout
69 Armour Wood Tank Sprinkler Wagon
70 Double Bob Farm or Business Man's Sleigh
71 4 passenger 2 seater Plan Box Body Bob Sleigh
72 Oblong Box Steel Tired Top Buggy
73 Oblong Box Rubber-tired Top Buggy
74 4 Passenger rubber-tired Extension Brougham or "Clarence"
75 Steel tired "C" Spring Gig
76 Rubber Tired Roof Seat Omnibus
77 4 Passenger Double Runner Bob Sleigh
78 Yellow Exercise Road Cart or Jogging Cart
79 High Wheel Farm Wagon with Box & Seat
80 1 Horse Wood Axel Light Farm Wagon
81 Unpainted Wood & Skein Axles Plank Dump Wagon
82 Farm Wagon with Bolster Springs
83 Single Seat Farm Bob Sled
84 F. Neumeister & Sons Grocery Delivery Wagon
85 "Oklahoma" Canopy Top Surrey
86 Double-End Reversible Extra Heavy Logging Truck
87 Milk Wagon
88 "Kingsbury" Stake Truck Case Goods Brewery Wagon
89 Side Spring Portland Cutter

90 J & W Jung Co. Delivery Sleigh
91 Portland Cutter
92 Oblong Box Steel Tired Top Buggy
93 Portland Cutter
94 Steel Tired Surrey Without Top
95 Steel Tired Paint Wagon
96 High Wood Hub Staggered Spoke Wheel Milk Wagon
97 Oblong Box Rubber Tired Top Buggy
98 Oblong Box Steel Tired Spindle Seat Runabout
99 Side Spring No Doors Portland Cutter
100 Red & Black Exercise Jogging Cart
101 Side Spring Portland Cutter
102 Portland Cutter
103 Oblong Box Steel Tired Top Buggy
104 Buck Board
105 Yellow Heavy Farm & Lumber Hauling with Cast Iron Bob Sled Runners
106 Double Seat 4 Passenger Democrat Wagon
107 Heavy Farm 2 Horse Bob Sled
108 Farm Wagon
109 Sheboygan Chair Co. Large Flat Bed Chair Truck
110 4 Passenger 2 Seated Double Runner Farm Bob Sleigh
111 Old Farm Bob Sled
112 3 Spring Handy Wagon
113 "Braasch Flyer"
114 Adult Size Rubber Tired Cunningham Hearse
115 North 8th Street Dairy Delivery Bob Sled
116 Extension Top Rubber Tired Phaeton
117 Cord Wood Wagon
118 4 Passenger 2 Seated Double Runner Farm Bob Sleigh
119 "B. Schmartz" Meat Market Wagon
120 Extra Step Democrat or Milk Wagon
121 Nickel Funeral Home Child's Hearse
122 Railway Express Agency Depot Baggage Wagon
123 Railway Express Agency Depot Baggage Wagon
124 Jump Seat Cutter
125 Portland Cutter
126 Otto Jung Coasting Bob
127 John Blazer Coasting Bob
128 Tuffy's Child Size Chariot
129 Oblong Box Handyman's Wagon

VII
Ornamental Wrought Iron Workers

CYRIL COLNIK

Cyril Colnik was born in 1871 in Triven, an Austrian village in the County of Steuermark. His earliest effort in his craft was when, at four years of age, he made nails for a dog house at a forge near the family estate in Triven where the Emperor Franz Joseph's horses were shod. He later studied at the Industrial Art School in Vienna, and, after extensive traveling as a journeyman in Europe, he came to this country in 1893 at the age of twenty to set up the German Government's iron works display at the World's Fair in Chicago. For that he provided a plaque as a commission and was awarded a gold medal; but since that Fair, like the New York Fair of 1966, lost so much money, he obtained merely a blue ribbon for it.

From the Chicago Fair, Mr. Colnik came to Milwaukee and established a shop on North Eighth Street between Wells and Kilbourn Avenues (see etching by Dr. George New). This

(page 138) Ornamental Iron Shop of Cyril Colnik, formerly on North 8th Street, between Wells and Kilbourn Streets, in front of the court house.

These "griffins," by Cyril Colnik, embroider the railings in one of Milwaukee's most widely known public buildings, the city hall. They were made of cast iron and then gilt bronzed.

was torn down in 1940 and a second ornamental iron shop was built at 531 No. Eighth, behind the home which his daughter still occupies.

Cyril Colnik died in 1941 and a sampler* of all types of wrought iron techniques is left with other examples of his work in his will to the city, but it and many other pieces so bequeathed are still cherished by his daughter Gretchen in their home on Eighth Street. The Germanic figure on the Brumder Building by Colnik, having been in his shop for eighteen years after being removed from the building, was sent in 1942 to Washington to be melted for use in World War II.

(opposite page) Early portrait of Cyril Colnik. Courtesy of the Milwaukee Public Library.

* See pages 223–224 *Wisconsin Heritage*, by Bertha Kitchell Whyte.

Wrought iron sign on the "Schlitz Brown Beer Hall," by Cyril Colnik.

Lamp by Cyril Colnik before the Schlitz Brown Bottle Beer Hall.

His work is widely distributed all over Milwaukee and other cities of the country, and a few of the sites taken at random are listed:

(1) Memorial Cross on altar at St. John's Cathedral.

(2) Ringling home in Sarasota, Florida.

(3) Insul and Ryerson homes in Chicago.

(4) The home of Herman Uihlein at 5270 North Lake Drive; three years work, which included door, stairway rails, chandeliers, fountain with marble bowl, marble top table.

(5) Grills of City Hall.

(6) Pieces taken from Pabst home, now used in Mader's Restaurant.

(7) Sign and lighting fixture, hardware at Schlitz Brown Bottle.

"Kavelage's Schloss," a seventy one year old mansion at 2431 West Kilbourn Avenue (old Cedar Street) was built in 1896 by Joseph B. Kavelage who commissioned Cyril Colnik to execute the balconies and railings on the house. The most impressive feature was the front porch supported by eight life-sized atlantes or male figures and surmounted by a Colnik railing. An ornamental balcony above it is shown here. The elegant parlor held a rococo chandelier of gilt bronze.

Mr. Clarence John Laughlin a New Orleans photographer and writer spent ten weeks wandering around Milwaukee, in which time he took 800 pictures, 400 of which he prepared for the exhibition in 1965 at the Milwaukee Public Museum, entitled *Old Milwaukee—Rediscovered.*

He was especially fascinated by what he called "fantasies of old Milwaukee" He said that Milwaukee had more fantastic things on its buildings than he had seen anywhere; columns, heads of angels, monsters, carvings in stone and wood—and wrought iron.* A monster by Cyril Colnik was featured in his exhibit and

* See article on "Camera Captures" in the Milwaukee Journal Sunday, Feb. 7, 1962.

is shown here. All of his pictures dealt with buildings erected between 1850 and 1920.

Unfortunately no list was ever kept of Colnik's commissions, but the variety and extent of his work as well as its artistic virtuosity established Cyril Colnik as one of the leading ornamental iron artists in the United States. Every piece of work was carefully designed at the drawing board before being executed. Mr. Gerhard Degner, of whom more will be written later, said, however, that an ornamental iron worker must use his imagination as well as skill and may change the design during forging, since in a drawing it is never possible to visualize what the finished product will look like.

Features by Cyril Colnik still remain after fifty five years,

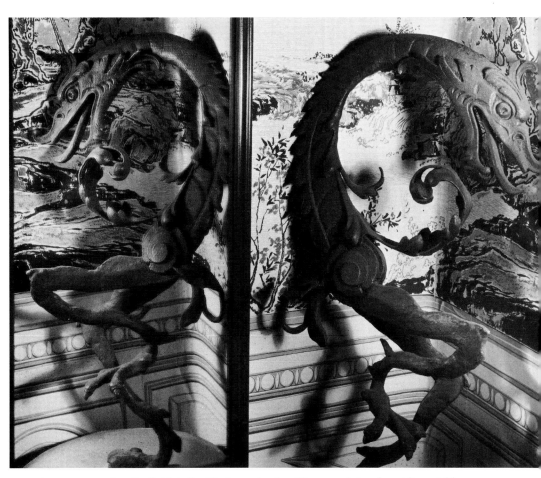

Capering monster by Cyril Colnik. Photographs by Clarence John Laughlin of New Orleans. Courtesy of the Milwaukee Museum.

(opposite page) Stairway, made by Cyril Colnik, of the mansion built by Herman Uihlein at 5270 North Lake Drive, Milwaukee. Photograph by E. M. Richardson.

145

in the building at 767 North Jefferson Street where George M. Niedecken presided as an interior designer and muralist who worked on Frank Lloyd Wright's early homes throughout the midwest. Mr. Niedecken often worked with Colnik who would supply all of the necessary ornamental iron work, such as latches, hinges, curtain rods for arched doorways, lanterns, radiator enclosures and even ash stands with marble columns.

Another well-known Milwaukeean with whom Colnik worked closely was the architect, Richard Philip, who designed Riverbend, the great home at Kohler, Wisconsin, of the first Walter J. Kohler who was Governor of this state.

I called upon Gerhard Degner, whose studio of Ornamental Iron Works is at 1023 West Center Street, hoping to hear what story he could tell about Cyril Colnik, whom he had known. No story evolved, for Cyril Colnik stuck strictly to his work, but I learned some interesting facts about Mr. Degner who, with his brother, William, are the last professional ornamental iron craftsmen in the Milwaukee area. They specialize in working with forging bronze which was once imported from Germany, but after Mr. Degner's father brought the formula for the alloy from Germany, the bronze was made in Milwaukee by the American Brass Company. It is of a golden bronze color, not yellow like brass, and can also be antiqued. The Degners use mostly forging bronze and aluminum.

The famous old cities of Savannah, Georgia, and New Orleans, have been noted for their iron fencing and grille work, but that had been predominantly of cast, not wrought iron, which is in contrast to the situation in Milwaukee. The Wearne Foundry in Mineral Point, however, did much cast iron work; railings, benches, etc.

Mr. Degner, when asked what he thought of our current welded sculpture, appraised it as *"junk"* and gave the opinion that

(opposite page) Cyril Colnik's balcony of the Joseph Kavelage home on Kilbourn Avenue, showing monster and angel heads. Photograph by E. M. Richardson.

not one of the so-called sculptors could forge a leaf or a scroll. He felt that forging was becoming one of the lost arts. He probably has not seen the interesting copper panel in Wausau, Wisconsin, made by E. T. Schoenberger for the First American National Bank, or the many other pieces of welded sculpture by our young welders.

There will never again be wrought and forging iron workers of the caliber of these old craftsmen as Cyril Colnik and Gerhard Degner. Collectors should take notice, for it is great fun to go Colniking.

(page 149) Fence and gate before 2640 North Terrace Avenue, formerly the home of William and Arthur Liebman. Wrought by Cyril Colnik.

VIII
Stained
and
Faceted Glass
Craftsmen

Introduction

Wisconsin has been singularly blessed with craftsmanship in the field of stained glass. However, before, introducing some of Wisconsin's most distinguished craftsmen in this field, it would be well to present a brief historical review of this long established historic craft including the recent development of so-called faceted glass.

Sir Herbert Read in his *English Stained Glass** gives the following broad period classifications of stained glass art:

1. The Age of Reason.

    The rise and fall of the Classical period of Christian art, generally known as Early Gothic, which was the truly great period of stained glass. (1150-1350)

2. The Age of Sentiment.

    The rise and establishment of humanistic standards. The Romantic or Late Gothic. (1350-1500)

3. The Age of Fancy (The New Renaissance).

    The humanistic decadence. The "Fanciful movements devoid of unanimity and religious sentiment." 1500 A. D. onwards.

(opposite page) Tiffany Windows in St. James Church, Milwaukee, in Memory of Anna Alice Smith. Signed by Tiffany in 1918. Dates March 14, 1856 and March 15, 1915. There are other fine examples of Milwaukee Tiffany windows in, Immanuel Presbyterian Church and St. Paul Episcopal Church.

* Read, Sir Herbert, *English Stained Glass*, Thames and Hudson, London.

Ruskin, in his *Stones of Venice*, says, "The perfection of a painted window is to be serene, intense, brilliant like flaming jewelry, full of easily legible and quaint subjects and exquisitely subtle harmonies; this perfection has been consummated in the designs, never to be surpassed, if ever again to be approached by human art, within the French windows of the twelfth and thirteenth centuries."

But Sir Herbert Read adds, "By the end of the fifteenth century Italian art had acquired the character of individuality. It had lost its universality, humility, its subordination to unity; all qualities of classic art. The era of romanticism was born." After that, stained glass windows were influenced by oil paintings and portraiture, coats of arms and secular windows.

In early times, as glass painting developed as an art, the church windows became the people's Bible, presenting the stories of the Holy Family and the Saints. Sir Herbert Read writes, "It would be true to say that between the middle of the 12th century and the middle of the 15th century this art (stained glass) was the supreme mode of communicating spiritual truths to the common people. This is not to forget the supreme position of architecture, but architects of the middle ages developed their style very largely in response to the clamant demands of the glass "painted."

In England the York Minster contained the earliest stained glass of the 12th century, and in France it was probably St. Denis Cathedral. The greatest windows of the Gothic Period are those of Chartres Cathedral, installed in the early 12th and 13th centuries, which still have most of their glass intact. In Paris, in a new spirit, were the famous windows of Sainte Chapelle dating about 1245.

Other cathedrals noted for their stained glass were Canterbury of England with its Old Testament themes and in France,

(opposite page) Trinity Episcopal Church, Wauwatosa, Design Erhard Stoettner, Photographer Richard Eels.

154

 ✳ SAINT DAVID ✳   ✳ SAINT OLAF ✳

the Cathedrals of Rheims, Bourges, Le Mans, Strasbourg, Laon and Tours. The great Gothic period lasted until about 1380. In the 15th and 16th centuries the windows were influenced by the Renaissance and more white glass was used which was then painted with enamels. Famous windows of that period are in the following Cathedrals: Sens, Auch, Beauvais, Gisors, Rouen, Evreux, Chalons-sur-Marne, Conches.

In the 17th century rectangular leaded sections were used with white glass painted with enamels. The process was called grisaille and the glass and architecture were not well related. The Reformation had demanded the removal of ornamental windows and hence the 16th and 17th centuries marked a decline of stained glass. In the 18th century the craft degenerated to its lowest level in developing stained glass as it was then mostly superficially painted for illustration. Overall design was neglected as was translucent blown glass.

1560 to 1789 was considered a decadent period of the art. A prominent example was a window of 1778 in New College Chapel, Oxford, designed by Sir Joshuah Reynolds depicting, "the Nativity," and the seven theological and cardinal virtues which Horace Walpole called "the washy virtues." It was popularly condemned. The period was devoted mostly to portraits painted on glass, and after that, stained glass was in eclipse until its revival in the 20th century.

In the 19th century there was some revival of the Gothic tradition and re-use of fine pot-metal glass (blown glass). William Morris (1839-1896) worked with the White Friars Glass Works in England to develop medieval glass, and artists such as Bourne-Jones and Rossetti developed cartoons, which was the technical name for the paper sheet with the full scale design. Morris popularized domestic stained glass production in England.

(opposite page) Trinity Episcopal Church, Wauwatosa, Design Erhard Stoettner, Photographer Richard Eels.

157

In the 20th century two fine English artists were James Hogan (1883-1948) and Martin Travers (1886-1948) who worked with the White Friars studios in England and in America where he designed five beautiful windows for St. Thomas' Church, New York. In the Harry Clarke Studios of Dublin, Ireland, glaziers were trained by Harry Clarke (1889-1931) and still produce very fine stained glass.

In the United States, well known studios are the J. R. Lamb Studios, the Cummings Stained Glass Studios, both of San Francisco, and the Chas. J. Connick Associates of Boston, besides several Wisconsin studios which will be discussed later in some detail. Louis Tiffany (1848-1933) created church windows incorporating the opalescent glass he developed, but he is better known for the use of glass in interior decoration and later for commercial objects, such as vases and lamps.

Charles J. Connick* indicates in *Adventures in Light and Color*, "The Renaissance of Gothic architecture in America through the apostolate of Messrs. Cram and Goodhue, marked the end of the opalescent enterprise (example—Tiffany glass). It conformed to the medieval laws of design under architectural control."

The Wisconsin craftsmen have drawn their inspiration from the periods of the Middle Ages, but designs have varied and with the faceted glass are generally abstract, following the spirit of the 20th century.

During all of this time the manufacture of stained glass and the technique of handling with installation in lead were the same, and, with the exception of faceted glass, the old methods are retained. Stained glass is blown in different countries according to the availability of ingredients, but none is blown for windows successfully in the United States. The whole supply has been dwindling on account of the scarcity of glass blowers. Also, glass

* Connick, Charles J., Adventures in Light and Color, Random House, N.Y. 1937.

is expensive and was once used as crown bullion (or money) in England and only for the nobility.* Crown bullion is a clear blown glass pane around the pontil point which gives off rainbow reflections.

However, judging from Czechoslovakia's fascinating glass exhibits at the Montreal Expo 67, glass blowing in Europe is becoming creative again and has resulted in marvelous productions, including fountains of glass.

Opaque substances, sand, lime and soda make up glass. They are melted in a pot, colored with metal oxides, and blown in a huge bubble, cooled and cut. Light passing through the glass gives it a surpassing radiance. Stained glass windows have been appropriately called "Cataracts of color between cliffs of masonry."

In making stained glass certain special sands coming from different European countries and metal oxides are used as the basic raw materials. For example, sand with cobalt oxide from Bohemia produces the clear bright blue color; with manganese oxide added, a violet color appears; with copper oxide, green tones are produced. Copper oxide alone produces a red so strong and dark it was added as a layer to clear glass for an overlay. Use of silver oxide in Germany produces a yellow color, and the brilliant flamboyant red glass made in France results when gold is added.

The effects of the early windows are of brilliant glass mosiacs. Besides biblical themes, the course of the years and signs of the Zodiac were shown. Grisaille work was used by the humble Cistercian Order showing gray or light colored glass with the designs done with the leading or black enamel painting. A stain might be painted on glass and fired to produce a yellow tone. Painting of features and drapery was done with a reddish brown or black powder which was later fused in heat of 1200 degrees.

*Erhard Stoettner fifty years ago bought some of the crown bullion glass in England and as a generous gift used the last of his supply for a window next to the author's front door.

A subject often used was "The Tree of Jesse," after an example in St. Denis Cathedral, showing a tree growing out of the body of Jesse, King David's father, with Christ's ancestors depicted in the branches and Christ crowning his family tree. Generally the high windows of the main aisle opposite the altar show motifs of Christ and Mary, while the side windows show narrative legends all in close relation to the stone architecture.

Faceted glass is a very recent development and was first produced about 1950 in the United States as more contemporary and was thus more easily incorporated with the architectural structure. It is made of slab glass, called dalles in Europe, generally of size eight inches by twelve and a full inch thick. The slabs are chopped or chipped by hand to provide reflecting surfaces, and when cut into pieces and embedded in cement or epoxy resin, give a brilliant as well as a strong window or wall. Lumps of glass can be inserted to produce certain effects.

There is good and poor faceted glass produced in the United States, but in some the epoxy can be as thin as the lead in stained glass work and becomes part of the design. Slab glass is now made in Germany, Belgium, France, England, and at the Blenko works in the United States in the State of Virginia.

In general the great advances of glass workers at the present time are in their cooperation with the architects. In addition to their glass work, the glass studios either design and execute the mosaics, metal and wood figures and altars, or they would design the pieces and then delegate the execution to craftsmen here or in Europe.

Wisconsin is fortunate in having four excellent studios where stained and faceted glass work of a very high order is being designed and produced. It is a pleasure to introduce several of the leading Wisconsin craftsmen in this field whose work is known nationally. Besides them, many young craftsmen are being trained, and Wisconsin's ecclesiastical work is very important in this country.

162

In a window, pieces of glass are bound together by strips of grooved lead (a cross section looks like an H), soldered at the joints and secured to the window frames by metal bars tied to the leads. The whole is fitted or re-enforced into the masonry by tee-bars.

(15) Window of Grace Episcopal Church, Sheboygan, Wisconsin, designed by Erhard Stoettner. Kohler Memorial Window, Christ the King Chapel.

ERHARD STOETTNER

Erhard Stoettner of Milwaukee was born in Bavaria, Germany, at Prien am Chiemsee in 1899, and is of the fourth generation of stained glass craftsmen. He was born in a home that was built over 200 years ago, which, in view of its history and architecture, has been placed under government restrictions which provide that no changes or additions are permitted to be made to this landmark. Mr. Stoettner's brother, Josef, still designs and executes stained glass windows within the ancestral studio of this old Bavarian home.

Erhard Stoettner started his apprenticeship at nine years of age, when, after school he would have to come home and go to work in the shop. In the summertime he would, on occasion, spend probably one month with an uncle who was a Monsignor in the Roman Catholic Church. This uncle insisted that all of his nephews read the books on art, astronomy, and history in his library. He gave them basic Latin, besides the history of the church, with the idea that some of the boys would become priests.

(opposite page) Lutheran Church of Norway, Wisconsin, designed by Erhard Stoettner.

On his school vacations, Erhard would work on some of the castles which abound in the mountain region of Bavaria and also on the famous Chateau of Mad King Ludwig the Second (on the Island of Chiemsee), which was patterned after Versailles. There he worked on the skylights of the roof. He can remember lying on Ludwig's bed, as a prank, while helping his father, who was employed in glass work at the Palace.

These magnificent palaces and castles inspired young Stoettner to follow the stained glass art as had his ancestors. At the age of fifteen he had joined the Bavarian Mountain Corps during World War I. In 1918 he was taken prisoner by the English but was released the same year.

Erhard Stoettner (associated with T. C. Esser Stained Glass Studios, Milwaukee), before one of his windows.

(pages 166, 167 & 168) De Sales Preparatory Seminary, 3501 South Lake Drive, Milwaukee. Erhard Stoettner made the windows, which were designed by the world-famous artist, Professor Anton Wendling, of the University of Aachen, Germany.

After the war, Erhard Stoettner returned to the stained glass profession and worked on churches in Luxembourg, Belgium, France and Germany, including the Cathedral of Chartres, to which people make pilgrimages just to see the famous windows. He worked five years on the post World War I restoration of the Cathedral of Rheims. This magnificent edifice was begun in 1211, and Erhard Stoettner worked with a family of stained glass workers who had taken care of the repair on the Cathedral for centuries.

In view of the magnificent architectural structure of the cathedrals in Europe, restoration work was continuous, and it took a whole generation, from father to son, to start from one side of the cathedral and end at the other. By the time they had finished restoration, another generation had to start all over again, not only on the stained glass windows, but also on the roofs and the delicate stonework. While working on the Cologne Cathedral, Erhard Stoettner attended art school and later obtained his degree as master craftsman at the School of Arts and Crafts in Duesseldorf, Germany.

Thoroughly indoctrinated in his craft, Erhard Stoettner came to the United States in 1931. After working in Boston and Minneapolis, he came to Milwaukee about 1934, and, at the suggestion of the late Archbishop Samuel Stritch of Milwaukee, established a stained glass studio in the manner of the old medieval concepts of stained glass with the T. C. Esser Company.

Mr. Stoettner's first big project in Milwaukee was to replace the glass in St. John's Cathedral after a fire. It was at the time of the depression and he had to work with inferior glass. (He says that one of the original windows should have been preserved in a Museum.)* Since then Erhard Stoettner has done outstand-

*The design for the stained glass in St. John's Cathedral in Milwaukee, executed by Erhard Stoettner was drawn by Leo Cartwright who died in the summer of 1967 in Ibberton, England. He was born in 1899 in Dublin, Ireland, and there studied art at the Harry Clarke Studio where he later became head designer. In 1927 he was hired by Charles J. Connick of Boston and while head designer there, produced one of his greatest works—the design of stained glass for The Cathedral of St. John the Divine in New York City. Leo Cartwright worked for the T. C.

ing work within eight cathedrals throughout the country as well as on some of the most prominent churches east to Pennsylvania and throughout the west. His work also includes stained glass for residences and inns, including the Mead Inn in Wisconsin Rapids and the Executive Inn in Sheboygan which incorporates Coats of Arms of countries from which many citizens of Wisconsin originated; Germany, Sweden, Norway, France, and Ireland.

For his work within the Basilica of Queen of all Saints in Chicago, he was given a citation by Pope John XXIII for creating stained glass windows of extraordinary beauty, design and craftsmanship. The baptistry murals and the mural in the Mother's Chapel, are works of art by Mr. Leo Cartwright of England, as associate artist. Mr. Stoettner says of this Basilica:

> One could spend all day in the Basilica, just in pure admiration of the design elements within the ceiling trusses and beams executed in 24 karat gold leaf, combined with tones of gray, ochre, terra cotta, resembling the ageless ornamentation within the famous Cathedrals in Europe.
>
> The Sanctuary catches your eye first as the focal point of the Basilica. Then the eye roams to either side, viewing the magnificently beautiful stained glass windows throughout the nave and transept, incorporating figures of Saints of many nations, Popes, the church at work, and intricate figure medallions within the transept windows depicting scenes from the Life of Christ, all combined to create one of the most beautiful and worshipful houses of prayer of our time.

Erhard Stoettner has also made stained glass and directed interior work in many a hand-crafted field stone and log cabin church from Wisconsin into the Dakotas, Montana, Wyoming, and other states where the parishioners have been poor but were able to incorporate the work of dedicated craftsmanship.

Esser Co. in Milwaukee from 1942–1951; and during that time in addition to working with Erhard Stoettner on St. John's Cathedral of Milwaukee, he designed the glass for the LaCrosse Cathedral. Later he continued his association from his studio in Carmel, California, until retirement to England in 1965. His work as a designer achieved national recognition.

Erhard Stoettner believes that the St. Joseph the Workman Cathedral, in La Crosse, Wisconsin, completed in 1962, represents Wisconsin's most magnificent. The glass work was executed by Mr. Stoettner. All of the interior decorative elements, the stained glass, mosaics, altars and bronze work were designed and made by craftsmen of Milwaukee, of which Mr. Stoettner says, "we, as Wisconsin craftsmen and artists, are very proud." It depicts the history of Christianity from the creation up to the time men brought Christianity into Wisconsin. The stained glass within the clerestory of this church incorporates over four thousand fishes, the fish being a symbol of the early Christians according to Christ's injunction, "I will make you fishers of men." The stained glass alone took three years to execute.

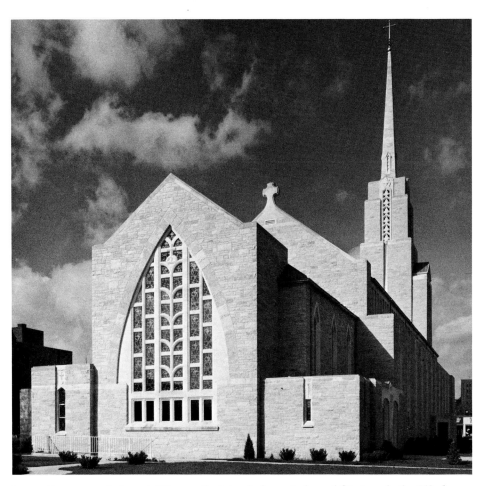

(opposite page and above) The south stained glass window of St. Joseph the Workman Cathedral, in La Crosse, Wisconsin, designed and executed by Erhard Stoettner.

173

Professor Anton Wendling of the University of Aachen, Germany who came often to Milwaukee, and whose work was recently celebrated in a monograph by the Minister of Cultural Affairs of West Germany, made the designs for clerestory windows, as well as the great south window, for St. Joseph the Workman Cathedral under the direction of Erhard Stoettner. He passed away in 1967.

Christ Episcopal Church, Whitefish Bay, Wisconsin, incorporates, in the stained glass, all English Saints within the clerestory, nave, and sanctuary. The lower aisle nave windows incorporate beautiful small intricate figure medallions depicting parables and miracles from the Life of Christ. There are about 160 figures in the *beautiful large east window* portraying other miracles and parables. Erhard Stoettner worked for two years on the designs and drawings alone, and on the east window the actual stained glass work alone took approximately six months. Mr. Stoettner cut every piece of glass himself.

Among many other works, Mr. Stoettner designed the windows for the Eisenhower Memorial Chapel at Kansas State University in Manhattan, Kansas, where the General's brother, Milton Eisenhower, was president at the time.

Mr. Stoettner was commissioned by his Excellency, The Most Reverend Karl J. Alter, D. D. Archbishop of Cincinnati, Ohio, to collaborate with the architect, Edward Schulte of Cincinnati, in the complete redevelopment of the Cincinnati Cathedral, St. Peter in Chains, from an exterior as well as an interior point of view.

The work within this Cathedral took approximately four years of labor, including the stained glass windows. Especially interesting was the window in the baptistry, executed of lustrous English Crown glass, which gives a kaleidoscopic color effect.

(opposite page) St. Joseph the Workman Cathedral, La Crosse, Wisconsin.

175

All of the intricate embellishments of ornamentation throughout the Cincinnati Cathedral including the trusses of the ceilings were designed and developed by Erhard Stoettner in gold leaf, with grays, whites, charcoal, terra cotta; in strict adherence to the Grecian architecture of the Cathedral. Many days of painstaking work in searching through his library for appropriate motifs were put into these design details to be transformed into full size, and executed by decorating craftsmen, creating an atmosphere of quiet, ageless beauty, and in its grandeur, "A Glorious Monument to God."

Mr. Stoettner maintains that well before the turn of the century, Milwaukee had been a leader in the ecclesiastical art fields, both in stained glass and later in faceted glass. The German people who settled in Milwaukee then were artists and technicians in this field—masters in stained glass, murals, mosaics, and wood carvings. They brought their medieval skills with them to beautify American churches and to create jewelled pictures in stained glass.

The Esser Stained Glass Studios have completed executing (1967) an exterior mosaic* for the Ascension Lutheran Church of Milwaukee on Layton Boulevard, depicting the Universal Christ, embracing the people of the world, all nations, trades and professions. The mosaic includes Martin Luther, for they were celebrating the 450th year of the Reformation. This mosaic, when lighted at night, creates a very dramatic appearance as seen by motorists on this heavily travelled thoroughfare.

Erhard Stoettner does not favor the faceted glass type of window, for his training was with the great stained glass windows of the 12th or 13th centuries, the techniques of which he has continued to this day. Today he works in conjunction with the T. C. Esser Co. in Milwaukee, where one can see all stages in the making of stained glass windows—the designing, cutting, glazing the pieces of glass into the lead, soldering, and painting. The second floor domain with its shelves of precious imported blown glass is a fascinating place often visited by groups of students.

* Mosaic is a composition of small pieces of Venetian glass.

Among other works of Erhard Stoettner in Wisconsin not mentioned before, are:

St. John de Nepomuc Church
  Milwaukee, Wisconsin
St. Jude Church
  Milwaukee, Wisconsin
DeSales Preparatory Seminary
  South Milwaukee, Wisconsin
St. Camillus Monastery
  Milwaukee, Wisconsin
Wisconsin Memorial Park
  Milwaukee, Wisconsin
Cardinal Stritch College
  Milwaukee, Wisconsin
Trinity Episcopal Church
  Wauwatosa, Wisconsin
Redeemer Lutheran Church
  Milwaukee, Wisconsin
Lake Park Lutheran Church
  Milwaukee, Wisconsin
St. Peter's Church
  Oshkosh, Wisconsin
Holy Family Convent
  Manitowoc, Wisconsin
St. John's Lutheran Church
  Merrill, Wisconsin
St. Anthony Church
  Lac du Flambeau, Wisconsin
St. Cloud Church
  St. Cloud, Wisconsin
Campion High School
  Prairie du Chien, Wisconsin
St. Dominic Church
  Sheboygan, Wisconsin
St. Coletta School
  Jefferson, Wisconsin

First United Lutheran Church
  Sheboygan, Wisconsin
First Methodist Church
  Ashland, Wisconsin
Grace Episcopal Church
  Sheboygan, Wisconsin
St. Henry Church (complete,
  with interior design)
  Watertown, Wis.
Holy Cross Seminary
  LaCrosse, Wisconsin
St. Joseph Church
  Fort Atkinson, Wisconsin
St. Mary's of the Lake Church
  Bailey's Harbor, Wisconsin
Our Saviour Lutheran Church
  La Crosse, Wisconsin
St. Paul Church
  Manitowoc, Wisconsin
St. Stephen's Church
  Stevens Point, Wisconsin
Zion Lutheran Church
  Wausau, Wisconsin
Sacred Heart Hospital
  Tomahawk, Wisconsin
St. Patrick Church
  Whitewater, Wisconsin
Peace Lutheran Church
  Oshkosh, Wisconsin
St. Thomas More Church
  LaCrosse, Wisconsin
Ascension Lutheran Church
  Milwaukee, Wisconsin

BERNARD O. GRUENKE

Bernard O. Gruenke, art director of Conrad Schmitt Studios, was born in Sheboygan, Wisconsin, February 17, 1913. After receiving his basic education at St. Peter Claver School and Sheboygan High School, he chose to further his art talent through intensive study and training at Layton School of Art in Milwaukee and later was awarded a scholarship to Corcoran Art School in Philadelphia. He also studied portraiture under Richardie of Philadelphia.

(opposite page) Head of Christ, by Bernard Gruenke.

Having completed his studies, and being an accomplished artist in his own right, he found considerable interest in and pursued the field of ecclesiastical art. He embarked on this career by becoming a member of the Conrad Schmitt Studios of Milwaukee in 1936, working closely with the founder, Conrad Schmitt, (1867–1940), who was born in Fussville, Wisconsin, and had started his studio in 1889. Since 1936 Bernard O. Gruenke has dedicated his life and resources to elevating the field of ecclesiastical art in this country. He used his extensive travels in Europe and Central America to study the architecture and art advancement in the old and new churches. The knowledge gained has been applied to promote and improve the caliber of American ecclesiastical art through works done by the Studio.

Mr. Gruenke is well known for his work in interior decoration. He has designed or redecorated the interiors of some of the largest and best known cathedrals and churches in the country.

As a result of his travels, Mr. Gruenke introduced and pioneered the use of faceted glass in this country. He began to experiment with the medium in 1950, with the first panels being cast at his home. Many of his panels toured the country on exhibition, demonstrating to artists and architects the new material and medium of glass that was now available. Mr. Gruenke was the first to recognize the great potential of this new medium and its application in today's architecture. He was not satisfied with merely perpetuating the traditional leaded glass art; he was anxious to progress—to adapt stained glass to the art concepts of today.

Mr.Gruenke has devoted much time, effort and money to research projects designed to advance faceted glass artistically and technologically (a search for a better epoxy, more durable panels and more refined production methods). Since its introduction, faceted glass has been used in thousands of churches and by artists and architects throughout this country and Canada. Many of these artists learned this new technique under the instruction

Bernard Gruenke.

and supervision of Mr. Gruenke himself. Mr. Gruenke had this to say about the progress being made in the medium:

There are many faceted glass projects in existence across the country; however, only a few of these can be called properly designed and executed. Many artists find it impossible to make the transition from designing stained glass to designing faceted glass. As a result, many of our faceted glass windows today are really leaded glass designs executed in slab glass and epoxy. In other words, the matrix is used merely as a thin slab joining agent, and not as an element of the design as it rightfully should be.

Admittedly, faceted glass is a difficult medium for an artist to work with—especially if his whole career has been devoted to work with stained glass. Faceted glass is a new medium, and the artist must re-educate himself with the new art concepts which apply to the designing of this glass.

181

In 1963 Mr. Gruenke was presented with the Award of Merit by the Wisconsin Chapter of the A.I.A. for outstanding achievement in the religious arts.

An outstanding example of liturgical design by the Conrad Schmitt Studio can be found in the charming stone church at

(opposite page and below) St. Mary of the Lake Church, Westport, Wisconsin, the artist-craftsman was Peter Recker of the Conrad Schmitt Studios, with decorations by the president Bernard O. Gruenke. (Photographer: A. J. Motelet, Madison, Wisconsin.)

Westport, a small community north of Madison in sight of Lake Mendota, which is named St. Mary of the Lake and embodies in it all the features of excellent modern craftsmanship. As the third church on the site (the second was burned by lightning in 1951) the eighty-six families, many of Irish extraction, began to build St. Mary of the Lake with architect Lewis Siberz and Bernard O. Gruenke as designer of the sanctuary appointments. Peter Recker, also of that Studio at the time, designed the stained glass windows and executed the mosaics, notably the Madonna suspended in the niche of the pylon, and the stations of the cross. The Rt. Rev. Monsignor Edward B. Auchter was in charge of the building and decoration of the church and to him must go much credit for its artistry.

The nave windows on the left (epistle) side show the missionary work of the various religious orders in Wisconsin, represented by the founders of those orders. The windows to the right or gospel side show the development of the Catholic Church in the immediate surroundings of Madison represented by the patron saints of·the church foundations in that area. Above the windows are the mosaic stations of the cross. One of the windows is of St. Albert the Great dedicated to Father Albert J. Mueller who was pastor of St. Mary of the Lake from 1905–1937.

These are of leaded stained glass, but the small rectangular windows used throughout are of faceted glass. The small faceted glass window in the baptistry, says Bernard Gruenke, is without a doubt the first piece of faceted glass produced and installed in this country. It was his first attempt to work at a medium which he had seen in numerous churches in Europe and which he was determined to initiate with his craftsmen here in America.

The altar is of black marble imported from Italy and behind it is a mosaic tapestry of black and gold centered by a six foot black marble cross.

The consistent artistry of this church of 400 parishioners is a tribute to their taste and devotion.

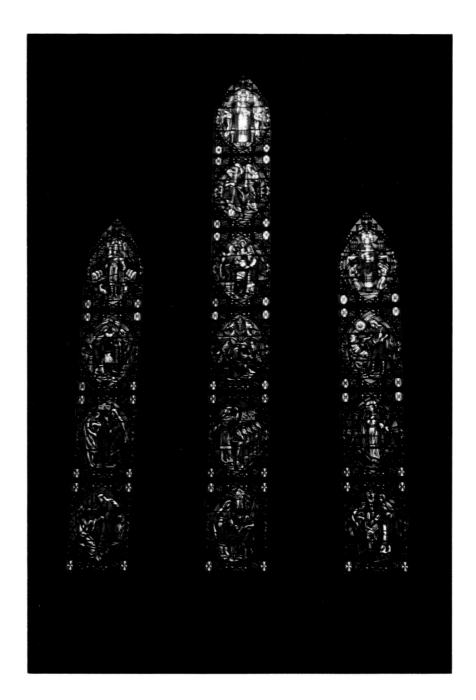

Christ Episcopal Church East Window. Whitefish Bay. Made by Erhard Stoettner.

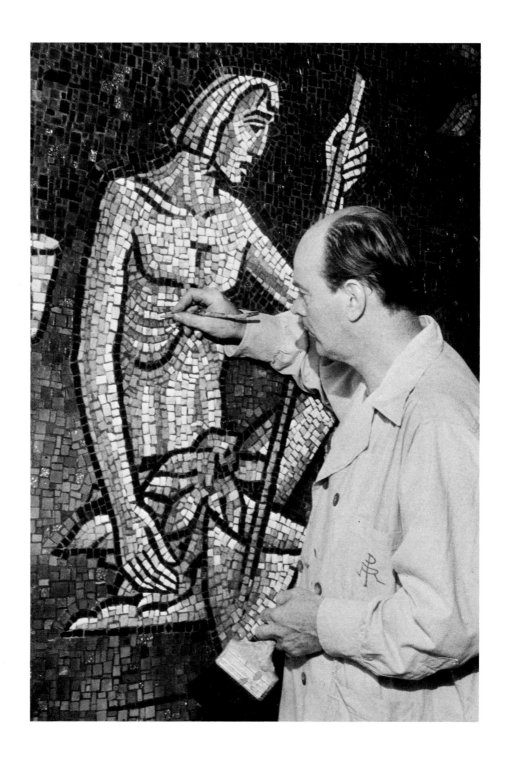

PROFESSOR
PETER RECKER

8833 Eichstatt, Adalbert-Stifter-Weg, 5 Germany

Peter Recker, who came to the U.S.A. in 1952 to paint a mural in St. Mary's Academy in Fort Smith, Arkansas, became associated with the Conrad Schmitt Studios from 1951 to 1958. In 1960, he was called back to Germany to execute some large works in stained glass windows and mosaics for various dioceses in Bavaria. In the United States he designed a mosaic behind the altar of St. Rita's Church in Indianapolis based on the negro spiritual "Swing Low Sweet Chariot." He also designed the stained glass windows for Zion Church in South Milwaukee, besides the mosaics and stained glass windows of St. Mary of the Lake in Westport.

(page 186) Professor Peter Recker, now working in Italy and Germany, was with the Conrad Schmitt Studios from 1951–1958.

St. Rita Church, Milwaukee, designed by Felix Senger, executed in faceted glass.

HELEN CAREW HICKMAN

Mrs. Hickman, a Wisconsin resident and stained glass artist, has been on the Conrad Schmitt Studios' designing staff since 1961. Her contemporary style in ecclesiastical design is well known nationally. Born in Erie, Pennsylvania in 1925, she obtained her degree at Carnegie Institute of Technology in 1947 and worked at the Hunt Stained Glass Studios in Pittsburgh from 1947 until 1951 and married Rolf Hickman in 1952. After working as a free lance designer, she joined the Conrad Schmitt Studios in 1961. Besides showing her work in many group shows and winning several awards, her commissions have included twenty-four churches in Pennsylvania, ten in other states, twelve in Wisconsin.

Both Mr. Gruenke and Mrs. Hickman qualify as artists, as well as craftsmen, but, as Mrs. Hickman said, "An artist cannot be divorced from his medium," which for them is stained and faceted glass.

At present, Mr. Gruenke is the owner and president of the Conrad Schmitt Studios, Inc. and spends most of his time directing and coordinating commissions secured by the Studio and in acting as a liturgical consultant for churches throughout the country. He presides over a beautiful office filled with examples of ecclesiastical art. The piece of honor is a large parchment missal of chants made in Coltrava, Spain, in 1452, but obtained by Mr. Gruenke in Mexico. There are bronze figures, candlesticks, paintings and a fine oriental rug. All over the building are stained glass pieces by the six designers employed in the Studio. The Studio is now located on a large plot in the vicinity of Waukesha where facilities have been enlarged and an exhibition room has been included. It is indeed a place to visit.

(pages 190, 191) St. Matthias Church of Milwaukee designed by Helen C. Hickman and fabricated by the Conrad Schmitt Studios. This will be the largest faceted glass window in the world. The architects were Darby, Bogner and Associates.

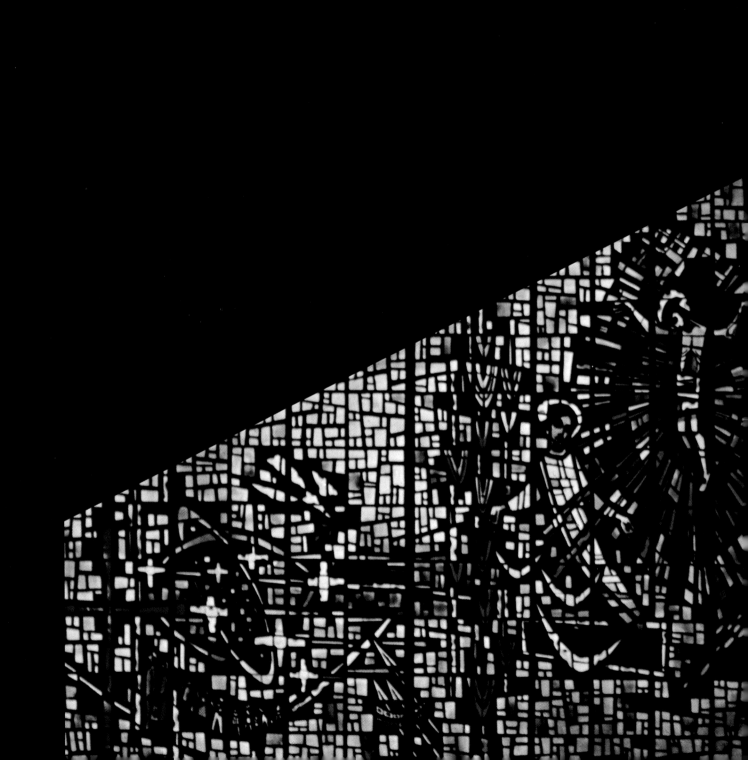

St. Matthias Church, designed by Helen Hickman, executed in faceted glass

CONRAD PICKEL

Conrad Pickel.

Conrad Pickel was born February 10, 1906, in Munich, Germany, and at fourteen years of age became a stained glass apprentice at the Franz Mayer Studio for twenty-five cents a week. Nowadays government regulations rule out apprenticeships, he says. His grandfather was a sculptor, and Conrad studied at the Art Academy in Munich but became fascinated with stained glass and chose that for his career. After his graduation he came to the United States in 1927 and worked in this country as a leading designer for many firms throughout the country. At length he came to Wisconsin to settle and for a time designed for a firm engaged in that field.

(opposite page) Stained glass window of Immanuel Presbyterian Church, which was made in Chicago.

However, Conrad Pickel wanted the freedom of working for himself and for a while worked as a free lance designer. He heard of a Minneapolis priest who was looking for a stained glass studio which could execute the windows for his new church. Conrad Pickel visited the priest, Father Rowan of St. Helena's Church of Minneapolis, who was doubtful about this craftsman because *he had no studio.* However after much discussion, the priest did allow Pickel to make a sketch. Father Rowan was much impressed with the sketch but was still quite worried since there was no studio to make the windows. He decided he would let Conrad Pickel make one window only on the condition that if he liked it he would have the parish pay for it. If he did not like it, however, he said that he would pay for it on his own and "smash it to bits."

Conrad Pickel then found an old barn near Waukesha where some young woodworkers had begun making church furniture. He rented the top floor, and there he began to work. The only way to get up to his studio was by means of an old ladder.

When the window was completed in this makeshift studio, Father Rowan flew from Minneapolis to see it. If he liked the window, Pickel was in business. Father Rowan came to the barn, climbed up the ladder, and looked at the window which was set up in two parts. He was silent for several minutes as he studied it carefully. To Conrad Pickel and his only employee, it seemed like hours. Finally Father Rowan beamed and said, "It is much more beautiful than I had dreamed possible."*

Conrad Pickel went on to finish the rest of the windows while more and more work began coming in. After working in his make-shift studio for some time, he built his present handsome studio next door, in New Berlin, Wisconsin. In addition, since 1956, he has maintained a studio at Vero Beach, Florida. He is

* This is from a letter by his son Paul Pickel written to the author telling the story about the beginning of his father's career.

194

there most of the winter where the only indication of a busy studio is a piece of stained glass sculpture in the garden.

Conrad Pickel has amazing versatality. Besides designing stained and faceted glass, mosaic work, painting and wood carving, he and his son Paul have developed a to-be-patented cement block with faceted glass inserts which they expect will provide myriad uses for builders and brighten many a structure.

In twenty years Conrad Pickel has designed and executed glass for hundreds of churches; twenty of them in Wisconsin, one in Puerto Rico, and some in Europe.

As in the medieval studios, Erhard Stoettner, Conrad Pickel, and Bernard Gruenke each have sons who work with their fathers, carrying on the fascinating craft of stained (and faceted) glass.

Faceted glass window by the Conrad Pickel Studios, Inc., New Berlin.

(pages 196 and 197) St. Mary Church, Waukesha, Wis. Designed by Conrad Pickel, executed in faceted glass.

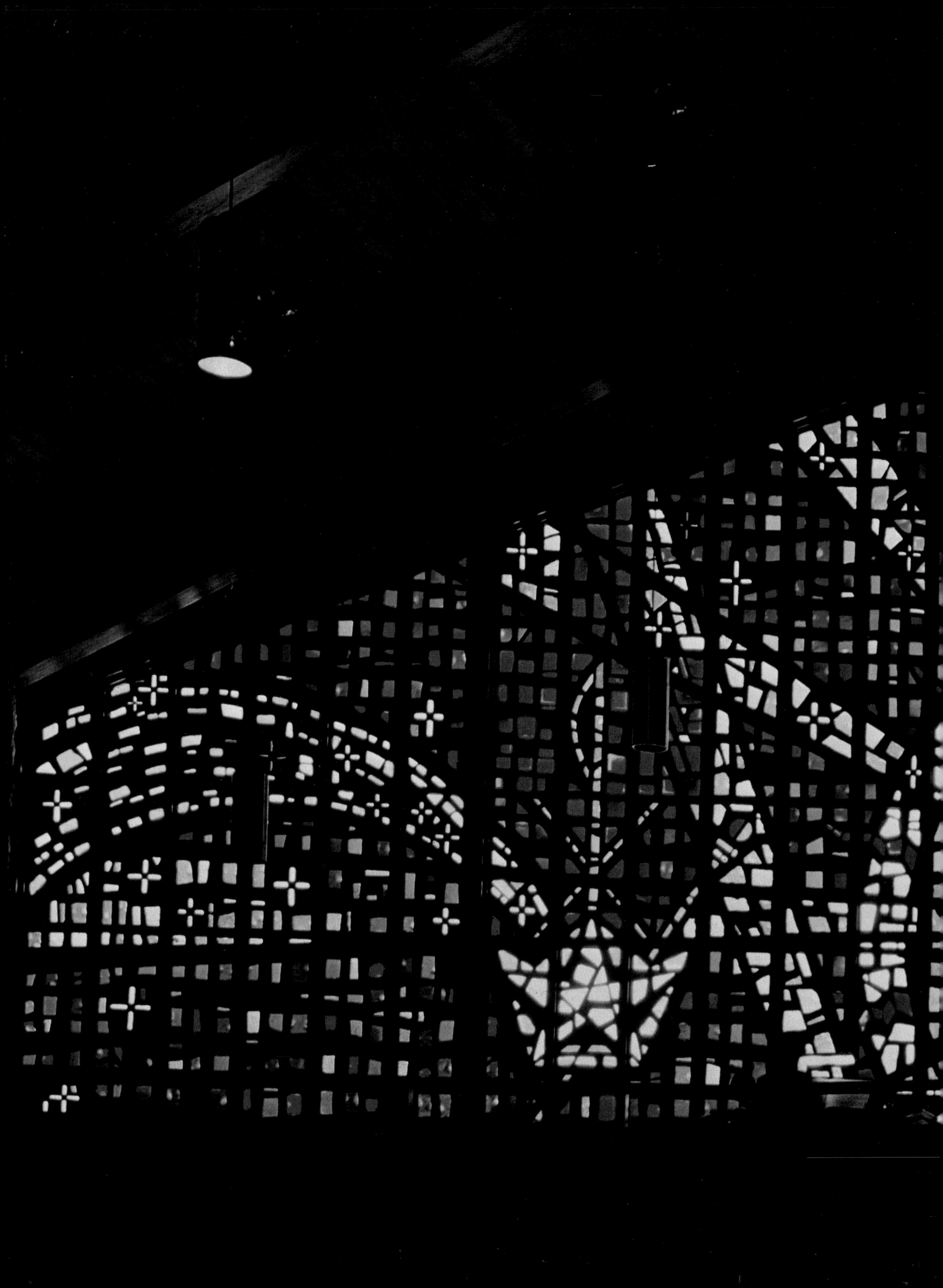

AUGUST M. GAVIN

The Gavin Mirror and Glass Works

The Gavin Mirror and Glass Works, also called Columbia Stained Glass Co., is located in an antiquated building on 1014 North Water Street, Milwaukee. The history of the building itself is interesting for it was first built as a hotel, deteriorated to a boarding house, then was a tobacco factory, later a horse hospital, and was finally a welding establishment at the time August M. Gavin (1882–1945) bought it in 1922 and started his own business.

(opposite page) St. Paul's Church in Green Bay, altar window, executed by the Gavin Brothers of Milwaukee.

Mr. Gavin had been working with Yahr-Lange of Bauch-Reichel Co. which had a leaded glass department. He bought out the department and named his new business the Columbia Stained Glass Co. It is now managed by his daughter, Miss Maggie Gavin, with her two brothers, Roman and Arnold, as craftsmen. At present they use free lance artists as designers.

About 1935 a display room was built upstairs which still has a high arched ceiling, Gothic fireplace with a mirror flanked on either side by small stone figures of St. Jerome and St. Peter under carved wooden canopies. This small display room is dominated by a beautiful large stained glass window which was designed by Karl Friedlmaier from Munich, Germany. In the center of the window is Christ the King with a crown, and on the right another figure of Christ with soldiers. A Madonna is on the left panel.

Gavin Mirror and Art Glass Works on 1014 North Water Street, Milwaukee.

On the first floor of the building, to which a front has been added, there is a labyrinth of rooms devoted to work tables and, in partitioned cupboards, sheets of dusty glass such as used to be imported by the carload from Europe. There are sheets of heavy drawing paper and a box of jewels which the brothers

200

found in the basement; moulded opalescent glass medallions which were used in Tiffany type windows. There is much Tiffany (opalescent) glass about and many period lamps of fifty years ago being repaired.

The company has created distinguished windows in many cities over the years and the brothers are still hard at work. Theirs is the oldest stained glass establishment in Milwaukee.

As a postscript to the foregoing studies of stained glass craftsmen, mention is hereby made of a lawsuit brought in 1924 between the Wagner-Larsheid Co. and the Fairview Mausoleum Co., both of Milwaukee. The Mausoleum objected that twelve stained glass memorial windows they ordered from sketches made by Frank E. Larsheid and executed by the Gustav van Treek Studios, Munich, Germany, were too dark and not with amber borders similar to windows in the corridor which had been accepted.

The twelve windows had been accepted by Mr. Thomas, president of the Fairview Mausoleum Co. but were later refused by the secretary, Edwin F. Pierce, after he discovered that the Wagner Larshied Co. had come under control of Conrad Schmitt, and his son Rupert. The Schmitts had requested payment for the twelve windows. Mr. Pierce said that he would have nothing to do with the Schmitts and had the windows removed. The Mausoleum won in the circuit court, but on an appeal, the State Supreme Court reversed the decision. In the opinion of Justice Marvin Rosenberry, April 6, 1926, the court found (190 Wis. 357) a full performance of the contract; that the windows were excellent from an artistic viewpoint and that recognizing the freedom permissible to artists, there was sufficient performance to enable the stained glass artist to be paid. (Two windows had been displayed before the court). This demonstrated the legal right of stained glass artists to exercise their discretion in creating designs and denied the right of a client objecting to said designs because of personal grudge.

Details of the reception room windows of the Gavin Columbia Glass Studios.

SUPPLEMENTARY STAINED GLASS BIBLIOGRAPHY

Armitage, E. Liddal, *Stained Glass*, Chas. T. B. Branford Co. Newton
    Centre, Mass. 1959.
Aubert, Marcel, *Le Vitrail Francais*, Editions de Deux Mondes, Paris,
    1959.
Hutter, Herbert, *Medieval Stained Glass*, Crown Publishers, Inc. N.Y.
Tiffany, Louis C., *Rebel in Glass*, by Robert Koch, Crown Publisher,
    1964–4, 6.
Brochure—*The Story of Stained Glass*, Prepared and Sponsored by the
    Stained Glass Association of America.

(opposite page) Reception room window of the Gavin Columbian Stained Glass
Studios, Milwaukee.

IX
Symbol
of the
Type of Craftsman

WILLIAM TE RONDE OF OOSTBURG

A story is told that when William Te Ronde, as a young man, took his regular job, he asked his employer at the end of the first day, "What shall I do tomorrow?" The employer said, "same thing." That did not appeal to young William so he quit then and there, and never, in ensuing sixty odd years, did he work for anybody but himself. Thus began a career which he carved successfully out of old fashioned individualism, always working and always doing something different.

When my family came to know him in his sixties, we were spending our summers on the beach of Lake Michigan in a cottage upon the construction of which five of the nine Te Ronde brothers labored—at fifty cents an hour. That was in 1937. William was the cabinet maker and it was then that I first learned of his versatility. He made the corner cupboards, bunks, shelves and acces-

(page 206) William Te Ronde with his model of a houseboat. "Author's."

sories, such as fireplace cranes. A lard bucket washed upon the shore which he bound with copper bands and topped with pine to make a table.

I must explain that Holland Township, Sheboygan County, Wisconsin, whose two villages are Cedar Grove and Oostburg, is inhabited almost entirely by people of Dutch descent, with only a few German farmers. On the nearby beach live those whom the local residents call picknickers or campers even though their cottages may have bathrooms and furnaces. The summer folk, whose outing garb is an eternal source of amusement to the villagers, buy provisions in two villages but never nick the solidarity or disturb the peace of these two groups of church-going people, who live self-respecting and economically-sound lives. Even the depression of 1933 didn't seem to affect them, they said.

William Te Ronde's house and shop on a main street of Oostburg.

The tranquility and self-sufficiency of the Village of Oostburg was epitomized in the eyes of the city-dwelling picknickers by Old William Te Ronde, whose large capable hands with their wrinkled carpenter's knuckles were always busy at their varied tasks in his workshop beside his home. His attire was invariably a shirt, a pair of baggy pants and a cap pulled down above a pair of twinkling eyes. "He must have a bald head," I thought, but never saw it. One Sunday we went to the Presbyterian Church in the village and were startled to see William dressed up and wearing a light brown toupee. His brother said he looked worse with it than without it. He had bought the wig in Sheboygan after some illness had caused him to lose all of his hair, even his eyebrows.

Trying to find the locale of William's first job and hoping to find how he sustained himself in his long independence, I visited his late brother George, who maintains a service station at the highway cross-roads, Poodles Corners, a few miles west of Oostburg. George was a craftsman himself, for besides being a pump and motor expert, he paints at pictures, decorates floats and once created a masterpiece of a paper cow for the county fair. When I told him that I was writing up his brother, Bill, as craftsman, George said immediately, "Well, he certainly was an independent fellow, but don't think that he was a saint because he wasn't one. When he was a boy he was plenty mischievous. He and I weren't especially friendly. Our brother Ben was his partner."

"What was the first job he had?", I asked. George replied, "Well, we lived on a farm. My folks settled here about a hundred years ago before there was a Sheboygan, an Oostburg, or even much of a Milwaukee. Father came to this country from Holland in 1858 when he was thirty years old and married right away. He bought a farm and built his own house with boards sawn by power from a windmill he built of wood. It had canvas sails. Father never learned English very well but we children learned to speak both Dutch and English. There were thirteen of us children, nine sons and four daughters. Times were plenty hard and when we boys were old enough father would say, 'You go over to our neighbors and saw wood.' Bill probably got 50 cents a day. There was nothing but woods all around. One of the first things that Bill and Ben invented was a kraut chopper for our mother. With thirteen children she had to keep something on hand."

I said, "How did he learn to do all of the things he did— iron work, machine building, carpentry, mill-work?"

"Oh," said George, "Just by trying. Bill was the carpenter of the family. He would make things smoother and better than the rest. He began dabbling in iron welding after watching a black-smith work. All of our lives, we boys had to do with machinery and my father boasted that none of us ever cut off a finger or toe."

Another brother, Henry Te Ronde, the plumber of the fam-ily, recollected that William first went to work for a carpenter named Brumels (later called Steyn). They made barns and then William got tired of barns. He wanted to build houses; so he did that for several years. After that William and Henry went into part-nership with a steam engine they bought and improved. They attached it to a threshing machine in the summer and used it for their sawmill in the wintertime.

They made many improvements on their threshing machine. Besides a sifter they devised a shaker attached to the apron similar to those on patented machines. Their shaker worked so well that farmers wanted one for their machines, but William would say, "No. This is just for us and is none of your business." When the boiler rusted William and Henry would take it apart and build it again with a part or two from Sheboygan. Their thresher ran per-fectly for twenty-one years while farmers around had exhausted two or three.

For their sawmill William built his own successful vertical power saw. When George was a boy he carried slabs for it and found it a "right hard job." There was a shed to house the engine and sawmill. William was the engineer and Henry did the sawing,

210

often with four assistants. But Henry contracted arthritis in the cold building and William bought him out. The building later was moved north of his home and was his workshop the rest of his life.

After the sawmill experience William and Ben experimented by building a windmill on top of the shed to power a gristmill. They had a lot of fun building it and it worked, but when the farmers came with their grain and the wind didn't blow, they had to give up the wind-powered gristmill idea. Henry said that while running the sawmill his brother William never kept books but could figure better in his head than he could on paper.

Still searching for the facts about that first job of William Te Ronde, I visited his brother Ed, of Cedar Grove, who had retired after being an undertaker for many years. His hobby was carving, mostly birds. Once he sold a number of his carvings to a wealthy man. Ed said, "Rich people will pay almost anything for something nobody else has."*

Although almost ninety years old, Ed Te Ronde still had a very sharp memory. He said that young William had a very enquiring mind and never lost it. A story of six year old Billy and a whistle shaped like a cigar, was told. Billy took it apart, but he couldn't put it together again and ended up crying in frustration, illustrating his persistence in pursuit of perfection. Later when he was in his teens he attempted to make a wheelbarrow which would not break. He used a three inch, iron truck tire, shrunk onto a wood frame with stout oak spokes. Then he would run the finished barrow as hard as he could against a beam on the side of the barn. If it broke in a certain place, Bill took it apart and made it over again, strengthening the part which broke. The other brothers throught that he was crazy, but he wanted the wheelbarrow to be indestructible.

Young Bill had very little schooling for he hated school like poison, Ed said. When he was in school, he spent all of his money

* I don't suppose that Ed TeRonde had read "The Theory of the Leisure Class" by Sheboygan-born Thorstein Veblen or had pondered about his doctrine of "Conspicuous Consumption."

for tools. He bought some boards which came from a fence of the Milwaukee, Lakeshore and Western Railroad when the boards were replaced with wire. With these he worked. At one time he worked all winter up in the shed without heat, making a bar for a tavern with thousands of pieces of wood inlay with various kinds of wood.

Whenever William saw something useful he would say, "That I can do, too." And he would make one just as good. He irked his brothers often by saying, "Why in the heck did you make it that way? It should have been done this way." The only thing that Ed Te Ronde could remember that stumped William was a machine that fastened wire mechanically around fish boxes, such as were used in the five fishing stations on Lake Michigan near the village. He never did perfect his attempted model, and the fishermen continued to twist on the wire by hand.

Ed told another story with much relish. After William was married (and it seems that he backed out of doing that many times but finally went through with it), he built a trellis for his wistaria vine and then carved a hawk to perch on it. His brother John saw it and said, "Why don't you get Ed to carve a good one?" William said, bristling, "That's all the darn fool can make—birds."

In later years people loved to visit the shop of Tinker Bill as he came to be known to his friends. It was fascinating just to learn what he was making any day. Once he was concocting a garden plow. Other times wonderful toys for our sons; decked river boats, rabbit hutches, cross-bows, an elaborate castle, car garages. As blacksmith, mill-wright, carpenter, cabinet maker, he could produce almost anything. In fact, in eighteen years I never knew him to be stumped at all. Every year he repaired furniture for us. Our antique tennis benches he mended often. In 1954 he made us a fine pine Welsh dresser from a little photograph. One day I met a nephew of his on the village street, and I said, "Randall, it must be wonderful for you to have an uncle as versatile as William Te Ronde." Randall said, "No, he won't do a thing for us; just says,

'Oh, go do it yourself.'" Each Te Ronde was supposed to be able to make anything.

Nothing intrigued old William more than a new project. At the time of the New York World's Fair, 1939, my husband brought home a magazine from the Soviet Exhibit showing a beach rocker as used on the shore of the Crimea. We took the picture to him and said that we would like just such a sand cradle. "Well," he said, "I never made one but I will do it." He said that every year about something, and he always made it.

One time a weaving class was to be started in nearby Port Washington, and the instructor brought him a picture of the looms she wanted, ordering fifteen of them. He told me about it and I said that I would like one, too, at the same price of $14.00— certainly a bargain for such a complicated affair. The instructor protested and said that he didn't have the right to make the same loom for me. That made Old William laugh. "Why," he said to her, "I knew Mrs. Whyte long before I knew you." That year William made about fifty weaving looms and then said that there was no money in it. The truth was that as usual he didn't charge half enough for them in the first place.

His little Dutch wife would have made a perfect model for Vermeer with her wide grey eyes and little pointed chin. She was shy and not as friendly and outgoing as Old William. Her hobby was lace-making and crocheting; even her rugs had crocheted edging. She had a weakness for making quantities of pillows and the corners were stacked high with them. You can imagine how decorated up the chairs were. One time when she was entertaining her church group, she intercepted a look of amusement cast by one of the members at her rugs. She never entertained again. My sons and I were in the shop one day on some errand and William said, "I have something in the house to show you." As we passed his little wife, one of the boys heard her whisper, "Don't give it to them." What he had to show was an adorable carved Dutch Windmill, beautifully painted. He didn't give it to us until after

she died. After her death, William, then almost eighty, tranquilly cared for his shop and his garden, cooked his meals, and kept his house in perfect order.

One Christmas we gave him an especially fine plane, whereupon at about age seventy he took up marquetry in a serious way, creating geometrical designs of different woods on frames, mirrors and table tops.

In the village I once saw him talking to a small group of children over the matter of some candy. He finished his discussion with them before speaking to us; their conversation was of utmost importance to him and we had to wait our turn.

As usual, in the early summer of 1956, I said, "We'll have to take it up to Old William." But there is an end of all good things. That spring, at eighty-five, William Te Ronde, that talented and delightful old gentleman, busy until the end, had hobbled up to a village store and collapsed against the counter.

Outside of our country we have the reputation of being commercial, interested only in profit; but I don't believe that our progress has been contrived only by individuals activated by acquisitive instincts. William Te Ronde never did spend much money for anything but simple tools and materials. At the time of his death everybody thought that he was hard up because he charged so little for what he did for people. But he left an estate of about $20,000 to his brothers and nieces and nephews. He seemed to me to have been a perfectly adjusted human being, who owed nobody and was perfectly happy making things, especially something that was a challenge. He had been a true individualist all of his days and the small village of Oostburg, although it had many personalities, considered him truly unique. When I consider how he could do so many things which a city-dweller would approach in absolute helplessness, I am led to think that these are the sort of folk who started this country on its fruitful way.

(opposite page) Model of a windmill by William Te Ronde. Photograph by Gerhard Bakker.

Index

Butlers, Samuel, 23

C. P. Kimball and Company, 124
Cabinet making, 13–23
Campion High School, 177
Canterbury Cathedral, 154
Cardinal Stritch College, 177
Carriage Association, 114
Carriage Journal, The, 114, 127
Carriages, 105–137
Cartwright, Leo, 170, 171
Cathedral of St. John the Divine, 170
Cellos, 55, 58–60
Chairs, 33
    three legged, 35
Chalons-sur-Marne Cathedral, 157
Chanet, George, 68
Charles C. West (ship), 100
Chas. J. Connick Associates, 160
Chartres Cathedral, 154, 170
Chests, antique, 30–40
Chippendale lowboy, 16
Christ Episcopal Church, 175, 185
Christy Corporatiton, 100
Cistercian Order, 161–162
Citizen (ship), 100
City of Midland (ship), 100
Clarke, Harry, 160
Cleaver Brooks Company, 115–119
Clement (ship), 99
Clicquenoi, Jake, 132
Clocks, organ, 19–23
Coachman's Horn, The, 114
Collins, Ivan L., 130
Colnik, Cyril, 139–148
Colnik, Gretchen, 140
Cologne Cathedral, 170
Columbia Stained Glass Company, 199
Concerto Walzers, 19–23
Conches Cathedral, 157
Connick, Charles J., 160, 170
Conrad Pickel Studios, Inc., 195
Conrad Schmitt Studios, 179, 180,
    183–184, 187, 189, 190–191
Courtland (ship), 92–93, 95
Craftsmanship, 9–11
Creative Intuition in Art and Poetry
    (Maritain), 11
Cudahys, John, 23
Cultural Wisconsin Day, 51
Cummings Stained Glass Studios, 160
Curry, John Stuart, 40
Darby, Bogner and Associates, 190–191
Davis, John, 23
De Smith, Ralph, 131

Decorative Art in Wisconsin (Foote
    and Smedal), 33
Degner, Gerhard, 145, 146–148
Degner, William, 146
Derleth, August, 40
DeSales Preparatory Seminary, 169,
    177
Dornbusch, Carl, 36
Downing, Paul H., 113, 127
Duiffoprugger, Gaspard, 61, 65

E. F. Klingler & Associates, Inc. 57, 73
Eau Claire Symphony Orchestry, 57
Eau Claire Wisconsin State University
    Fine Arts School Library, 65
Edmunds, Mrs. Nora, 29–30
Edward L. Ryerson (ship), 100
Edwards, Joseph, 100
Eells, Richard, 23, 38, 40, 154
Eirich, Rudy, 130
Eisenhower, Milton, 175
Eisenhower Memorial Chapel, 175
Emil F. Klingler, Inc., 73
English Stained Glass (Read), 153
ERB Memorial Building, 130
Esser Stained Glass Studios, 176
Evening Star (ship), 95
Evreux Cathedral, 157
Executive Inn, 171

Faceted glass, 151–203
Fairview Mausoleum Company, 201,
    200–201
First American National Bank, 148
First Methodist Church, 177
First United Lutheran Church, 177
Fitch, Captain, 89
Fitch, Grant, 77–79, 81
Folk Arts of Norway (Stewart), 30, 31
Fontanne, Lynn, 26, 36
Foote, Anne, 33
Fossum, Gladys H., 33
Fox, Chappie, 115
Frank, Glen, 40
Franz Mayer Studio, 193
Fraser Shipyards, Inc., 100
Friedlmaier, Karl, 200
Frizzell Coach and Wheel Works, 112

Gaar, John, 13–23
Gaar, Mrs. John, 15
Gaar, John, Jr., 15, 17
Gaar, Joseph, 15, 17
Gaar, Leo, 15, 17
Gaar, Mary, 15, 17

218